Pre-Algebra Brain Teasers

Author:

Lorin Olschanski

Introduction

Pre-Algebra Brain Teasers was created by a mathematics teacher. The activities are designed to be used as self-teaching tools for students. Students can solve problems and obtain immediate feedback from each activity. These activity sheets should only be used as supplemental materials for the objectives being taught in the mathematics classroom.

This book is divided into three sections:

Brain Teasers— The activities in this section cover 13 pre-algebra topics.

Student Guide— These reference pages are provided to help students as they work through the brain teaser activities. You may wish to reproduce pages 79–99 for the students to keep on hand as they complete the brain teaser pages.

Answer Key— Students can use this section to check their solutions.

Special thanks to the following students who played a part in putting this book together: Tara Harris, Corey House, Rachel Opland, Nick Rinehart, Amy Shadowens, Jennifer Stark, and Diona St. Charles.

Teacher Created Resources, Inc.
6421 Industry Way
Westminster, CA 92683
www.teachercreated.com
ISBN-1-57690-039-8

©1999 Teacher Created Resources, Inc.
Reprinted, 2005
Made in U.S.A.

Editor:
Mary Kaye Taggart

Cover Artist:
Larry Bauer

Table of Contents

Table of Contents *(cont.)*

Amazing Face (I)

Directions: Using order of operations, solve each problem below. Then, starting at the face, use your answers, in order from 1–20, to find a path to the outside of this number maze. (Always choose the closest correct answer.)

1. $(100 \div 2) - (6 \times 8) =$ _____

2. $(100 \div 2) - (6 \times 8) + 2 =$ _____

3. $3 + 28 \div 7 =$ _____

4. $3(14 - 6) =$ _____

5. $(82 \div 2 - 16) \div 5 =$ _____

6. $(16 - 3)(18 \div 9) =$ _____

7. $84 \div 12 \times 7 - 18 =$ _____

8. $\dfrac{96 - 41}{66 \div 6} =$ _____

9. $\dfrac{37 + 38}{30 - 25} =$ _____

10. $(52 - 4) \div 6 =$ _____

11. $\dfrac{17 + 13}{19 - 13} =$ _____

12. $2(4 + 5) - (6 \times 3) =$ _____

13. $3(2 + 6) - 3 \times 5 =$ _____

14. $(9 \div 3) + (4 \times 7) - (20 \div 5) =$ _____

15. $[(10 \div 2) \times 3] - (2 \times 6) + 3 =$ _____

16. $2[(8 - 5) + (4 + 2)] =$ _____

17. $3[2(4 + 1) - 3 \times 2] =$ _____

18. $4[2(4 \div 2)] - 3^2 =$ _____

19. $(3^2 - 5) - (4 \div 2) =$ _____

20. $2[(3 + 1)^2 - 5 \times 3] =$ _____

8	4	7	24	8	4	15	33	25	29	18	2	8	15	31	7	11	12	3
6	2	7	6	18	3	33	31	26	24	1	9	7	10	26	6	5	4	9
2	7	9	27	0	6	15	5	8	5	7	9	7	26	31	5	15	8	5
8	6	4	2	0	8	12	3	☺	2	4	6	8	10	12	4	16	18	2
0	8	7	6	5	9	10	4	3	4	8	10	9	7	8	9	10	7	8
5	5	3	26	1	2	27	8	2	4	7	15	2	11	19	3	21	22	3
14	8	5	6	7	8	9	6	10	6	7	15	6	31	2	0	10	13	4
11	2	7	12	18	6	9	16	18	15	5	25	4	2	0	3	11	17	8
27	1	6	8	5	0	5	18	12	14	23	4	5	31	27	2	16	21	2
0	26	7	9	28	6	5	15	13	7	29	9	6	4	26	5	13	15	4
3	27	8	19	2	3	8	13	8	2	32	8	2	11	12	6	19	28	1
9	6	5	7	22	0	7	15	4	2	4	7	7	41	52	5	27	29	0

Focus: Solving problems using order of operations

Amazing Face (II)

Directions: Using order of operations, solve each problem below. Then, starting at the face, use your answers, in order from 1–20, to find a path to the outside of this number maze.

1. $(\frac{1}{3} \times 6) + (-2 \times \frac{1}{2}) = $ _____

2. $-\frac{9}{20} \times 120 - 6 \times (-\frac{1}{3}) = $ _____

3. $-8.4 \div 2.1 + \frac{33}{11} = $ _____

4. $3.9 + 5.1 - 6.4 \div .8 = $ _____

5. $[1.6 - (-4.4)] \div (-2) = $ _____

6. $(6.8 + .7) \div (.25 \div .5) = $ _____

7. $2\frac{5}{8} + 3\frac{11}{24} + 4\frac{11}{12} = $ _____

8. $(\frac{5}{6} + \frac{3}{12}) \times \frac{24}{13} = $ _____

9. $(-\frac{3}{4})^2 \div \frac{9}{16} + -3 = $ _____

10. $1\frac{1}{3} \div \frac{2}{3} - (-1 - 6) = $ _____

11. $\left[(-2 \div -\frac{1}{3}) \times -8 \right] \div -12 + -3 = $ _____

12. $(3.05 - 1.36) \div .13 = $ _____

13. $[(\frac{5}{9} - \frac{5}{18} + 1\frac{13}{18}) \div -\frac{44}{11}] \times 8 = $ _____

14. $\dfrac{(4.7 + 1.6) \times 5 - .5}{-3} = $ _____

15. $2\frac{1}{2} - \frac{2}{3} - 1\frac{5}{6} = $ _____

16. $\dfrac{9^2 \div (4 + 5 - 12)}{9} = $ _____

17. $\dfrac{(2\frac{1}{3} + 1\frac{2}{3})}{-4} + \dfrac{4}{16} \times \dfrac{64}{4} = $ _____

18. $\left[\dfrac{21}{30} \div \dfrac{(-7)^2}{15} \right] \div \dfrac{-1}{14} = $ _____

19. $-\left[\left(\dfrac{2}{3} + 1\dfrac{1}{3} \right) \div \dfrac{1}{6} \right] + \dfrac{10}{5} = $ _____

20. $\dfrac{(-9.31 + -.05)}{-.9} + (-9.6) = $ _____

0	-3	7	-52	1	-3	-3	15	-48	43	7	-3	15	-8	21	-5	1	-1	9	-6	-4	-16
-27	-5	4	-6	11	28	11	2	1	24	-19	1	-15	11	-3	3	-13	52	-10	2	17	-5
14	-3	0	9	-41	36	9	-2	2	-17	18	-1	15	-14	2	0	20	-1	4	22	-4	8
-5	10	9	28	17	8	1	1	54	13	-52	8	-14	17	-2	11	-10	3	-8	3	-3	-10
-4	20	8	2	3	32	-1	13	-9	☺	1	-3	14	-14	9	-4	4	-15	-3	12	-13	-20
-3	-19	7	-2	30	33	52	1	0	5	-2	9	-14	11	-10	1	-4	-11	0	-9	9	11
-2	-18	6	9	2	8	-4	11	51	-4	3	20	33	-9	-7	-2	13	-35	8	59	-43	0
-1	-17	5	1	29	-46	0	-3	-53	10	-10	-4	-34	-3	0	21	19	1	43	57	-8	14
0	16	4	13	1	9	-2	1	-52	-1	1	-5	22	17	8	-35	0	6	-5	-2	7	-12

Focus: Solving problems using order of operations

Name That Term

Directions: Look at the definitions and examples below. Think of the mathematical term which best describes each. Find each term in the puzzle. The answer to number one has been circled for you.

```
A E Q U A T I O N N N I O N T I O N
A C S S E V I T A I C O S S A B C
S N O I T A R E P O F O R E D R O
E E O C I R I N V E R S E S R A M
S T C N O I D I E E V I A I T C M
E N O S Y A E N S R N T C M E K U
H E M T T B N O I S S E R P X E T
T S M R I L T R O F O N L L P T A
N N U E L E I E R E P E B I R S T
E E T V A D T R S A N K A F E T I
R P O N U E Y T P S O C I Y S R V
A O R I Q I N V E X I A R B S E E
P R O P E R T I E S E R A U I D A
I O N S N D I S T R I B V S V R D
R O P D I S T R I B U T I V E O D
```

1. (2 + 3) + 6 = 2 + (3 + 6)

2. 6 x 1 = 6

3. a + b = b + a

4. [ ]

5. ( )

6. the symbol used to take the place of an unknown

7. a mathematical sentence that contains an equal sign

8. an equation which contains a variable

9. a combination of variables and numbers and an operation

10. the order in which you solve math problems

11. another name for mathematical rules

12. 3 (2 + a) = 3 x 2 + 3 x a

13. to make easier or reduce

14. the opposite—These operations undo each other (like + and -)

15. a sentence with a <, >, <, or > sign

Focus: Defining algebraic terms

"Express" Yourself

Directions: Translate each phrase into an algebraic expression. Once translated, find the expression in the puzzle and draw a line through it. In the puzzle you will connect problems 1–4, then stop, connect problems 5–7, then stop, connect problems 8 and 9, then stop, and finally connect problems 10–12. When all of the expressions are found and the lines are connected correctly, you will spell a word.

1. 5 more than D
2. Twice a number W
3. The product of 60 and W
4. A number, N, decreased by 18
5. 14 minus a number, M
6. Twice a number, C, plus 6

7. Three times N decreased by 8
8. The sum of a number, R, and twelve
9. The quotient of N and five
10. Fifteen divided by Z
11. 3 decreased by a number, A
12. A number, M, decreased by 49

3	J	–	I	+	–	B	+	18	+	D	I	x
(	D	÷	14	3	x	(	26	+	N	)	A	I
4	2	+	÷	4	60	A	B	14	÷	x	÷	x
x	D	x	6	x	N	+	60	x	17	–	14	H
T	+	–	W	+	–	+	E	N	+	÷	–	T
+	5	)	÷	÷	18	Z	÷	R	18	B	+	18
9	(	4	(	2	÷	T	+	10	)	P	H	÷
)	+	x	F	x	)	D	U	21	(	Q	)	C
D	÷	14	x	–	6	3	7	36	7	x	U	–
8	+	S	+	+	–	3	+	Z	(	22	60	)
+	+	x	C	14	–	M	x	N	E	x	÷	E
T	x	x	0	+	O	K	+	N	9	÷	W	–
3	2	D	F	N	2	29	47	K	–	60	–	H
+	–	4	3	–	18	(	46	W	+	8	60	+
M	4	x	÷	A	–	Y	C	B	x	W	÷	49
A	N	N	R	+	12	Y	Y	÷	10	+	–	–
+	–	–	+	N	÷	÷	92	84	2	Y	W	M
3	8	8	V	÷	x	÷	48	59	21	3	+	81
x	x	x	–	5	+	(	)	15	M	+	N	M
N	3	3	+	15	–	N	21	÷	3	–	A	–
L	–	19	÷	÷	x	20	E	Z	F	+	–	49
L	÷	6	x	12	+	N	÷	16	K	(	10	)

Focus: Translating phrases into algebraic expressions

Lipstick Lady

Directions: Find the letter for the expression which matches each phrase. To answer the riddle box question, write the letter on the blank space or spaces that match the problem number.

1. A number added to 6	(D) 9 – n
2. 10 decreased by a number	(R) 18 ÷ n
3. 21 plus a number	(E) 21 + n
4. A number divided by 18	(H) 10 – n
5. Four times a number	(N) n + 11
6. Four times the sum of a number and two	(A) 4n
7. 18 divided by a number	(Y) n – 3
8. A number minus 3	(O) 2n
9. A number decreased by 10	(S) 6 + n
10. 11 more than a number	(W) n ÷ 18
11. A number subtracted from 3	(G) 3 – n
12. A number multiplied by 2	(I) n – 10
13. The sum of 9 and x	(T) 4 (n + 2)
14. The quotient of 9 and a number	(K) 9 ÷ n
15. The product of 9 and a number	(U) 9 x n
16. 9 less than n	(M) 9 + x
17. A number subtracted from 9	(P) n – 9

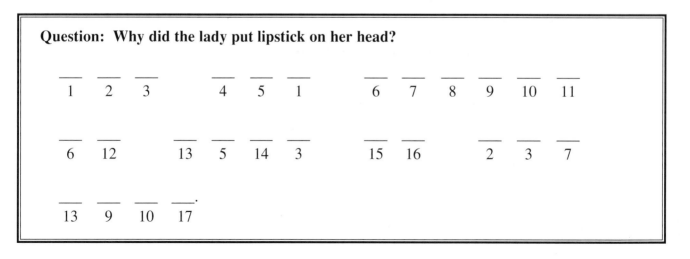

Question: Why did the lady put lipstick on her head?

___ ___ ___   ___ ___ ___   ___ ___ ___ ___ ___ ___
1 2 3   4 5 1   6 7 8 9 10 11

___ ___   ___ ___ ___ ___   ___ ___   ___ ___ ___
6 12   13 5 14 3   15 16   2 3 7

___ ___ ___ ___.
13 9 10 17

Focus: Identifying expressions

Writer's Dilemma

Directions: Use the information in the magic boxes to answer the question at the bottom of the page. A magic box is a figure in which the sum of each column and row is the same. Using the values for x, y, and z in magic boxes 1 and 2, evaluate the expressions found in the Model Magic Box. After writing the answers in the correct boxes, look at the blank spaces below. If an answer is below one of the blanks, write the letter found in the box with the answer on the appropriate blank space. Finally, total each row and column. Every total should be the same, and that will be your magic sum.

Model Magic Box

x+y+2z	3x+z	y+3z	x+2y
x+y+z	x+y+4z	3x	2y+z
2x+y+3z	x+2y+z	x+y	x+2z
x+y	y	x+2y+3z	3x+3z

Magic Box #1: x=1, y=2, z=3

G	A	N	C
A	H	S	Y
F	V	S	Y
S	O	D	R

Magic Box #2: x=4, y=3, z=5

E	E	I	W
R	M	R	N
L	H	Y	D
Y	S	T	M

Question: Why don't journalists always enjoy their meals?

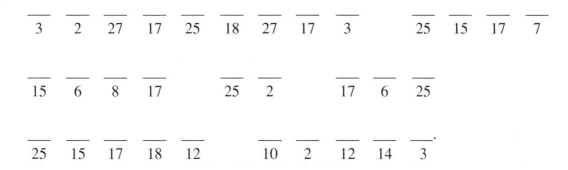

```
___  ___  ___  ___  ___  ___  ___  ___  ___      ___  ___  ___  ___
 3    2   27   17   25   18   27   17    3        25   15   17    7

___  ___  ___  ___       ___  ___       ___  ___  ___
15    6    8   17        25    2        17    6   25

___  ___  ___  ___  ___       ___  ___  ___  ___  ___.
25   15   17   18   12        10    2   12   14    3
```

Focus: Using variables and evaluating expressions

A Really "Pig" Show

Directions: Name the property shown by each statement. Below the blanks in the question box are sets of three problem numbers. Two of the three problems in each set have the same property for an answer. The other is different. In each blank write the letter of the single different property.

Equations

1. $3 + 5 = 5 + 3$_____
2. $2 + (4 + 8) = 2 + (8 + 4)$_____
3. $a + 0 = a$_____
4. $a \times b \times 1 = a \times b$_____
5. $a(b + c) = a \times b + a \times c$_____
6. $(m \times 3) \times 2 = (3 \times m) \times 2$_____
7. $(5 + y) + 1 = 5 + (y + 1)$_____
8. $(14 + 8) \times 0 = 0$_____
9. $t + 12(n + 1) = t + 12 \times n + 12 \times 1$_____
10. $18r + 18q = 18(r + q)$_____
11. $(5 \times 6) \times 7 = 5 \times (6 \times 7)$_____
12. $0 = r \times 0$_____
13. $(c \times d) \times e = (d \times c) \times e$_____
14. $(p \times q) \times r = r \times (p \times q)$_____
15. $48 \times 1 = 48$_____
16. $11 = 11 + 0$_____
17. $(t + r) + s = t + (r + s)$_____
18. $45 \times (9 \times 8) = (45 \times 9) \times 8$_____
19. $(12 + 4) + 6 = 6 + (12 + 4)$_____
20. $n \times r + n \times t = n(r + t)$_____

Properties

A. Commutative Property of Addition
B. Commutative Property of Multiplication
I. Associative Property of Addition
M. Associative Property of Multiplication
H. Identity Property of Addition
T. Identity Property of Multiplication
P. Multiplicative Property of Zero
U. Distributive Property

Question: Before the pig went on stage to do his comedy routine, he was given some very important advice. What was it?

_____ _____ _____   _____ _____   _____ _____!
1, 3, 19   1, 6, 14   4, 15, 18   3, 16, 17   4, 10, 20   1, 2, 9   7, 8, 17

Focus: Identifying properties of multiplication and addition

A Sensible Solution

Directions: Write <, >, or = in each circle. Then discover the hidden outline in the puzzle by starting at the point by the star. Connect this point to the greatest number from next problem. Continue doing this for numbers 1–20. When looking for each answer, always choose the closest available point with that answer. If you have an equation in which both sides are equal and neither side is "greater than," you are only expected to connect the line to a point of that value once. After you have finished connecting the lines for numbers 1–20, do numbers 21–25 according to the directions below. Once you have finished the picture, solve the riddle by copying in order the letters of the points your line went directly through in order, to solve the riddle below.

1. Begin at ★ .
2. 3 ◯ 5
3. -3 ◯ 5
4. -3 ◯ 3
5. -4 ◯ -8
6. -2 ◯ 0
7. -6 ◯ -5
8. -1 ◯ -2
9. |-7| ◯ 7
10. |-6| ◯ 8
11. |-9| ◯ 8
12. |-3| + |2| ◯ 4
13. |-1| + |-2| ◯ |8| + |-3|
14. |-15| - |8| ◯ |-2| + |4|
15. 12 ◯ 0
16. -13 ◯ 0
17. |13| ◯ -13
18. |2 + 5| ◯ |-7|
19. |-3| x 2 ◯ 4 x |1|
20. 2 + |5| + 4 ◯ 3 (|-4|)

For items 21–25, put the numbers in order from least to greatest. Continue connecting the points by using the ordered numbers.

21. (-13, -5, 0, -8, 1)
22. (-6, -18, -10, 3, -2, 2)
23. (1, 0, -7, -3, -10)
24. (-22, -11, -12, -5, -18, 7, -15, 0, 2, 3)
25. (-6, -5 -4, -3, 0,-1, -2)

Question: What would a frog do if he could not find scissors to cut a coupon out of the newspaper?

____ ____ ____ ____ ____ ____
1st letter   2nd letter   3rd letter   4th letter   5th letter   6th letter

Focus: Comparing and ordering integers

"Spl-Integers"

Directions: Solve each problem. Starting on the top line, connect the answers from this page onto the next page. Then, starting at problem 21, write ten problems that involve the addition of integers. Formulate the problems so that their answers will complete the symmetrical picture on the next page.

1. $4 + (-4) =$ _____

2. $-1 + (-3) =$ _____

3. $3 + (-4) =$ _____

4. $-19 + (-6) =$ _____

5. $-13 + 6 =$ _____

6. $-6 + 13 =$ _____

7. $-8 + (-13) =$ _____

8. $-5 + 18 =$ _____

9. $0 + (-2) =$ _____

10. $-26 + 86 =$ _____

11. $99 + (-22) =$ _____

12. $-18 + (-35) =$ _____

13. $-86 + 14 =$ _____

14. $21 + (-3) + 8 =$ _____

15. $36 + (-8) + (-3) =$ _____

16. $-81 + 96 + (-1) =$ _____

17. $-46 + (-37) + 8 =$ _____

18. $51 + (-53) + (-8) =$ _____

19. $-14 + 86 =$ _____

20. $-6 + 91 + (-3) =$ _____

21. _____

22. _____

23. _____

24. _____

25. _____

26. _____

27. _____

28. _____

29. _____

30. _____

Focus: Adding integers

"Spl-Integers" *(cont.)*

-3	100	-73	54	0	4	83	-58	-15	94
	-100	-35	44	-4	-8	32	-75	-37	-36
-62	-34	31	-1	64	-22	-16	-1	-11	46
	-75	-14	-25	-7	1	-50	-45	-3	-15
-61	51	-59	7	6	-19	97	-9	-57	3
	-60	-51	-21	73	75	23	8	95	85
-14	84	13	-2	-20	5	96	-33	-18	84
	65	93	60	6	31	41	56	91	-5
-63	8	77	30	-59	3	82	-47	-12	-13
	92	-53	-72	26	-75	-10	72	-17	86
91	-43	-62	-34	63	-73	2	-6	57	54
	-5	-41	-52	25	14	-38	55	-100	2

A Military Matter

Directions: Solve each problem. Use the letters next to the problems to solve the riddle at the bottom of the page. Many letters will be used more than once while other letters will not be used at all.

H. 7 + (-5) = _____   **Q.** -7 – (-3) = _____   **Z.** (6 - 2) – (-4) = _____

Q. -8 + 4 = _____   **X.** -15 + (-6) = _____   **N.** 6 - [2 - (-3)] = _____

D. 4 + (-6) = _____   **S.** -19 – (-18) = _____   **M.** 6 + [2 - (-4)] = _____

B. -15 + (-3) = _____   **A.** 7 – 16 = _____   **I.** 10 + 22 + (-7) + (-30) = _____

F. -28 + 28 = _____   **V.** -2 – (-8) = _____   **P.** -31 + 62 + (-9) = _____

G. |-9| – |2| = _____   **U.** 8 – (-3) = _____   **T.** 9 + 24 + (-5) + (-25) = _____

O. 6 + -9 = _____   **E.** -9 + (-7) = _____   **R.** -5 + -6 + -9 = _____

W. -7 + -8 = _____   **Y.** -2 + 7 = _____   **L.** |-20| + |-19| - 2 = _____

K. -2 + (-4) = _____   **J.** -18 + (-3) = _____   **C.** 5 x 3 – (8 – 6) = _____

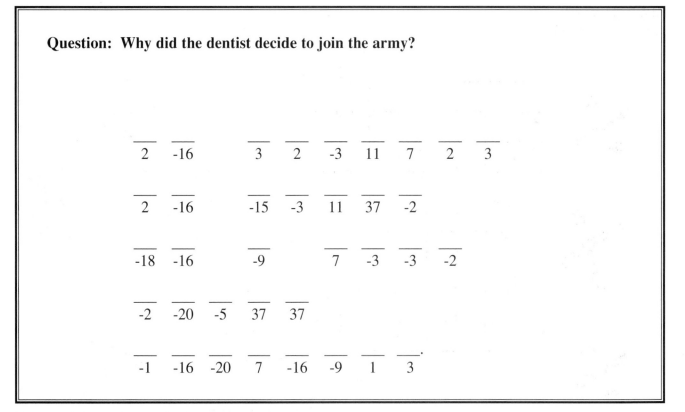

Question: Why did the dentist decide to join the army?

$\overline{}\ \overline{}$ $\overline{}\ \overline{}\ \overline{}\ \overline{}\ \overline{}\ \overline{}\ \overline{}$
2 -16   3 2 -3 11 7 2 3

2 -16   -15 -3 11 37 -2

-18 -16   -9   7 -3 -3 -2

-2 -20 -5 37 37

-1 -16 -20 7 -16 -9 1 3 .

Focus: Adding and subtracting integers

Puzzling Problem

Directions: Solve each multiplication or division problem below. After you solve a problem, write the numbers in the boxes provided in the cross number puzzle. (There is one space provided for each number.)

Across

1. 362 x -2
2. 102 x 3
3. -784 ÷ -4
6. 3419 ÷ -13
7. -11,180 ÷ -26
9. (1475 x - 4) + 3
11. -1170 ÷ -18
12. (-289 x 45) + (-121)
15. 2^3 x 2^2 x -2 x -3 x 10
16. -5 x 6 x -3 x -21 x 10,000
17. -630 ÷ 30
19. -2700 ÷ -30
20. (-2 x -4) x 10,563
21. -259 x 4
23. -696 ÷ (-58)
24. -221 x (-3)
25. -2 x -2 x -43

Down

1. -1462 ÷ 2
4. -1254 ÷ -6
5. 5592 ÷ 12
6. -26 x 956
8. -65,975 ÷ 25
9. 1124 x -5
10. (-156 x -2) -5
12. (-12 + -16) x 4
13. -117 ÷ -3
14. -35 x -36 x 10
17. 4598 ÷ -22
18. (2^3 x 5^3) + |-8|
21. -(2^6) x -18 x -100 + -10
22. 360 ÷ 15
25. - 4 x (-18 + 58)
26. (-196 x -4) + -21
27. (-2242 x 2) ÷ (-19 x 1)

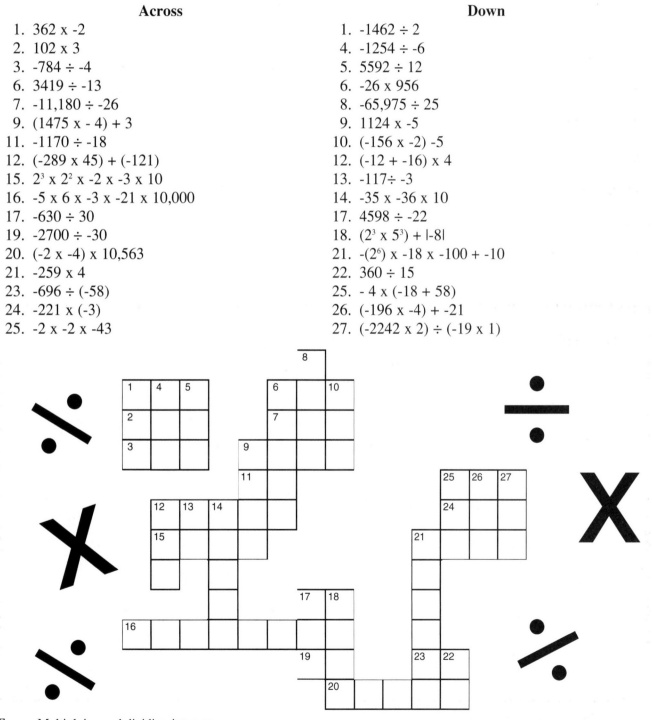

Focus: Multiplying and dividing integers

Too Fast!

Directions: Solve each inequality. To solve the riddle below, write each variable in the blank above its answer.

1. I + 8 ≤ 6

2. V - 6 > 8

3. N - (-3) < 20

4. 3U > 69

5. -13S < -195

6. A ÷ 7 ≥ -112

7. 17M ≥ -102

8. -13E ≤ -91

9. B ÷ -14 < -11

10. R ÷ -3 ≤ 5

11. 8T ≤ -120

12. H ÷ 21 > -12

13. 22C ≥ -352

Question: What caused the elderly man to walk so fast?

___ ___　　 ___ ___ ___ ___
≤-2　≤-15　　　≥-6　>23　>15　≤-15

___ ___ ___ ___　　 ___ ___ ___ ___
>-252　≥-784　>14　≥7　　　>154　≥7　≥7　<17

___ ___ ___
≤-15　≥-252　≥7

___ ___ ___ ___ ___　　—　 ___ ___ ___ ___
>-252　>23　≥-15　≥-15　≤-2　　　≥-16　≥-784　<17　≥7

Focus: Multiplying and dividing integers

Lovesick

Directions: Analyze each equation, and determine what should be the next step in solving the problem. Solve each equation. Next to each equation are three choices. Each choice shows a first step and an answer. To solve the riddle find the choice which contains both the correct step and correct answer, and write its letter in the blank above the number for the problem.

1. $x + 9 = 18$ (R) $-9, x = 27$ (S) $-9, x = 9$ (T) $-18, x = -9$

2. $x - 13 = 16$ (H) $+13, x = 29$ (I) $+13, x = 3$ (A) $-16, x = 29$

3. $b + (-6) = 6$ (E) $+6, b = 12$ (O) $-6, b = 0$ (N) $-6, b = 12$

4. $b + (-12) = 21$ (R) $+21, b = 33$ (S) $-12, b = 9$ (T) $+12, b = 33$

5. $n + (-5) = -23$ (A) $+5, n = -18$ (O) $+23, n = -18$ (I) $+23, n = 28$

6. $y + (-8) = -12$ (N) $+8, y = -20$ (S) $-8, y = -20$ (K) $+8, y = -4$

7. $m - 27 = -63$ (A) $+27, m = -90$ (E) $+27, m = -36$ (O) $+63, m = -36$

8. $x - (-26) = 55$ (N) $+26, x = 91$ (S) $-26, x = 29$ (D) $-26, x = 91$

9. $y + (-47) = -74$ (N) $-47, y = -121$ (S) $-47, y = -27$ (T) $+47, y = -27$

10. $-33 = h + 16$ (H) $-16, h = -49$ (R) $+33, h = 49$ (O) $-16, h = -17$

11. $15 = a + 17$ (A) $-17, a = 2$ (E) $-17, a = -2$ (I) $-15, a = 2$

12. $5 + n = -13$ (N) $-5, n = -8$ (T) $+13, n = 18$ (S) $-5, n = -18$

13. $-13 + k = -37$ (N) $+13, k = -50$ (T) $+13, k = -24$ (L) $-13, k = -50$

14. $-11 + r = 29$ (O) $+11, r = 18$ (A) $+11, r = 40$ (I) $-29, r = 40$

15. $-23 = t - 81$ (D) $+23, t = -58$ (R) $+81, t = 58$ (I) $+23, t = 58$

16. $-8 + m = -22$ (T) $+22, m = 14$ (R) $+8, m = -30$ (E) $+8, m = -14$

17. $q + (-9) = 14$ (D) $+9, q = 5$ (S) $+9, q = 23$ (T) $-14, q = -23$

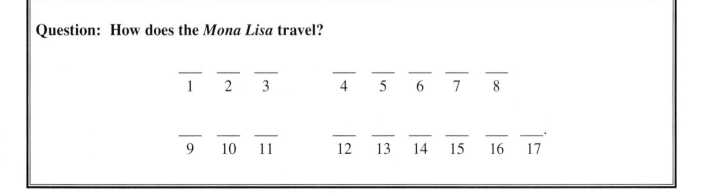

Question: How does the *Mona Lisa* travel?

___ ___ ___   ___ ___ ___ ___ ___
1   2   3   4   5   6   7   8

___ ___ ___   ___ ___ ___ ___ ___ ___.
9   10   11   12   13   14   15   16   17

Focus: Solving equations using the addition or subtraction steps

A Croaking Crook

Directions: The puzzle below is filled with equations. Items 1–10 are all answers. (You will not use all the answers.) Begin this activity by searching for equations to match the answers. When you find a match, look in the Step Box to find the step which you took to solve the problem. Then, once you have found the step, notice the letter next to it. Place this letter on the blank line in the riddle which corresponds to the problem just solved.

1. y = 1	6. y = 6	
2. y = 2	7. y = 7	
3. y = 3	8. y = 8	
4. y = 4	9. y = 9	
5. y = 5	10. y = 10	

Step Box

A = add 5	**K** = divide by 8
B = multiply by 3	**L** = subtract 2
C = add 3	**M** = divide by 7
S = divide by 6	**N** = multiply by 8
E = subtract 7	**R** = subtract by 5
H = multiply by 5	**D** = subtract 20
I = divide by 3	**T** = divide by 5

```
3   3   -   6   +   5   =   4   2   1   +   -   1   3   10  7   9
+   19  2   6   -   5   y   10  +   2   13  =   =   4   y   3   8
-   14  y   +   5   =   10  6   y   x   8   =   8   +   50  -   y
2   +   -   -   ÷   4   =   +   5   14  =   10  3   =   20  +   y
15  ÷   3   3   5   9   ÷   6   x   3   6   3   5   11  +   -   +
3   ÷   =   +   y   =   5   8   ÷   4   x   x   12  11  16  4   20
15  y   6   3   4   =   3   9   -   y   y   y   +   7   +   =   =
=   x   9   x   6   3   x   y   =   99  ÷   x   +   10  y   3   26
16  18  5   3   y   +   y   4   y   1   3   5   7   =   9   -   =
+   =   2   7   +   =   =   +   8   +   -   5   =   =   6   +   2
y   39  14  y   6   8   12  ÷   9   4   5   3   2   7   21  x   x
=   1   =   -   x   ÷   y   6   y   +   7   =   14  x   19  =   y
36  10  +   2   y   -   x   ÷   x   3   2   y   +   20  =   40  3
```

Question: Why did the frog go to jail?

__	__		__	__	__	__	__	__	__	__	__
4	10		1	7	5	3	4	10	10	7	6

__		__	__	__	__	__!
8		9	5	4	3	7

Focus: Solving equations using the inverse operation

The Wacky Werewolf

Directions: The puzzle below is filled with inequalities. Items 1–11 are all answers. Begin this activity by searching for inequalities to match the answers. When you find a match, look in the Step Box to find the step which you took to solve the problem. Then, once you have found the step, notice the letter next to it. Place this letter on the blank line in the riddle which corresponds to the problem just solved.

1. y < 1
2. y > 2
3. y < 3
4. y > 4
5. y < 5
6. y > 6
7. y < 7
8. y > 8
9. y < 9
10. y > 10
11. y < 11

Step Box	
A = divide by 6	**L** = subtract 30
D = multiply by 3	**N** = add 0
E = subtract 18	**O** = subtract 5
G = divide by 4	**R** = divide by 20
H = add 6	**W** = subtract 16
I = multiply by 2	**Y** = subtract 7

```
y   +   >  20  <   y   -  21   >  48  36  <   -  16  17   x
x  26   y   ÷   y   +  18   <  34   +   4   >   5  49   ÷   x
<   <   x   1   -   8   ÷  27   >   x   <   y   ÷   2   >   3
y  13   8   <   6   >  20   3  19   ÷   y   +   x   7   ÷  63
-   ÷   <   -   <  40   x   <   >   9   x   7   6   7   ÷   y
0   y   6   +   5   y   y   +   5   <   6   <  15  19   <   +
>   y   ÷   <   ÷   2   >   x   8  18   <  12  24  51   3  30
4  25   x   3  12  18  40   ÷   6   7  67   -   <   +  27   <
>   >   <   >   y   -   3   +   8   <   >   y   +   6   >  37
16  12  12   x   ÷   <  31   >   x   -  18   ÷   -   9  14   <
+   +  11   +   3  16   +   x   y   +   +  13   x   +   y  21
y   <   >   ÷   >   x  18   ÷   <  23   3   y   +  16   >  26
<   >   y   x   4   >  32  10  49   +   y   x  22   <   2   >
```

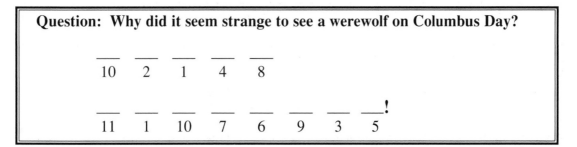

Question: Why did it seem strange to see a werewolf on Columbus Day?

$$\overline{}_{10} \ \overline{}_{2} \ \overline{}_{1} \ \overline{}_{4} \ \overline{}_{8}$$

$$\overline{}_{11} \ \overline{}_{1} \ \overline{}_{10} \ \overline{}_{7} \ \overline{}_{6} \ \overline{}_{9} \ \overline{}_{3} \ \overline{}_{5}!$$

Focus: Solving equations using the inverse operation

Follow the Divisibility Road

Directions: Find your way from start to finish through the maze by evaluating each expression, using the assigned values for a, b, c, d, and e. If your answer to a problem meets the requirements of the clue, draw an arrow to the problem. Then write the matching answer next to the clue. The first one has been done for you. When you have completed the first five, add your answers together, and check the sum to see if you are taking the correct path. (**Hint:** You will only move up, down, or horizontally.) Continue to check the sum of every five answers. When you have made it through the maze, total your four sums together. They should equal 824.

$$a = 1 \quad b = 2 \quad c = -2 \quad d = 8 \quad e = 13$$

Clues

_____1. divisible by 2 and 4
_____2. divisible by 13
_____3. divisible by 2
_____4. divisible by 5
_____5. divisible by 3 and 5

Total = 101

_____6. divisible by 2, 3, and 6
_____7. prime number
_____8. divisible by 7
_____9. divisible by 11
_____10. divisible by 2 and 3

Total = 212

_____11. divisible by 7
_____12. divisible by 3
_____13. divisible by 3 and 5
_____14. divisible by 3 and 5
_____15. divisible by 9

Total = 175

_____16. prime number
_____17. divisible by 5
_____18. a negative number
_____19. divisible by 4 and 8
_____20. prime number

Total = 336

Start
↓

$6 + c$	$3c + d$	$e + d$	$14a + e$
$23 + a + b$	$-(bcd - 14)$	$2d + a$	$be - d$
$e - c$	$d - c$	$a + b + c + d + e$	$100 - ac$
$4d + 2b$	$e + 2b$	$37 + c$	$(d - a)^2$
$3e$	$b + c + 73$	$23 - c$	$2e + d + 5$
$12 + b - a$	$c - 49$	$b + 11 - c$	$5(e - 2b)$
$c - b$	$a + b + 19$	$3(a + d)$	$3b$
$17 + c$	$e - a$	$d + e + c$	$e + d - 3$
$a + 4$	$c - a + 2$	$a + 104$	$a + b + c$
$e - d$	$d \times e \times b$	$-6c$	$2b + 2c$

Finish

Focus: Using the divisibility rules while evaluating expressions

Time for a Treat

Directions: Solve each problem below. Each answer must be a prime number. Find the answer in one of the circles on page 22, and notice the letter by your answer. To answer the riddle question below, write that letter on the line above the number of the problem that you solved.

Problems

1. (-3 x -25) + (-4)

2. (-13 + -16 + -30) x -1

3. -6 x 5 + 61

4. (-50 ÷ 2) x (-2) + (-3)

5. -3 + 30 + -6 + 22

6. -2 x –25 x 2 – 3

7. (-68) ÷ (-4)

8. (-25 ÷ 5) x (-19 ÷ 19)

9. 75 + (-18) + (-7) + 3

10. 152 + (-26) + (-13)

11. 43 – (-7) + 17

12. (-3 x -30 + 1) ÷ 13

13. (108 ÷ 3) + 64 + 17 + (-10)

14. -3 x 6 + 24 + (-4)

15. -1 + (-72) ÷ (-3)

16. 28 – [42 ÷ (-7)] – 42/2

17. 3 + 4 x 26 + (-4)

18. -84 ÷ 4 + 40

19. 20 – 30 ÷ (-3) – (-2) + (-3)

Question: When is a candy bar a tasty drink?

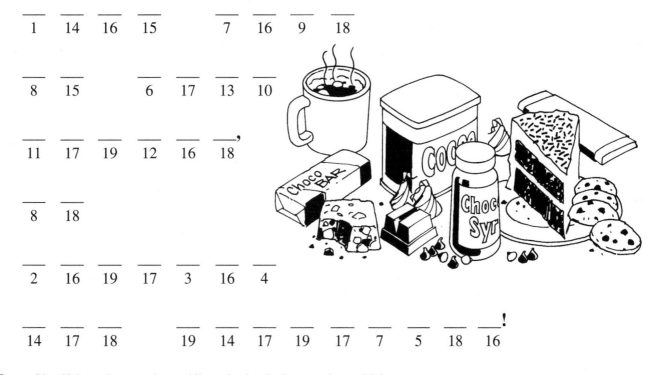

$$\overline{}_{1} \;\; \overline{}_{14} \;\; \overline{}_{16} \;\; \overline{}_{15} \qquad \overline{}_{7} \;\; \overline{}_{16} \;\; \overline{}_{9} \;\; \overline{}_{18}$$

$$\overline{}_{8} \;\; \overline{}_{15} \qquad \overline{}_{6} \;\; \overline{}_{17} \;\; \overline{}_{13} \;\; \overline{}_{10}$$

$$\overline{}_{11} \;\; \overline{}_{17} \;\; \overline{}_{19} \;\; \overline{}_{12} \;\; \overline{}_{16} \;\; \overline{}_{18},$$

$$\overline{}_{8} \;\; \overline{}_{18}$$

$$\overline{}_{2} \;\; \overline{}_{16} \;\; \overline{}_{19} \;\; \overline{}_{17} \;\; \overline{}_{3} \;\; \overline{}_{16} \;\; \overline{}_{4}$$

$$\overline{}_{14} \;\; \overline{}_{17} \;\; \overline{}_{18} \qquad \overline{}_{19} \;\; \overline{}_{14} \;\; \overline{}_{17} \;\; \overline{}_{19} \;\; \overline{}_{17} \;\; \overline{}_{7} \;\; \overline{}_{5} \;\; \overline{}_{18} \;\; \overline{}_{16}!$$

Focus: Identifying prime numbers while reviewing basic operations with integers

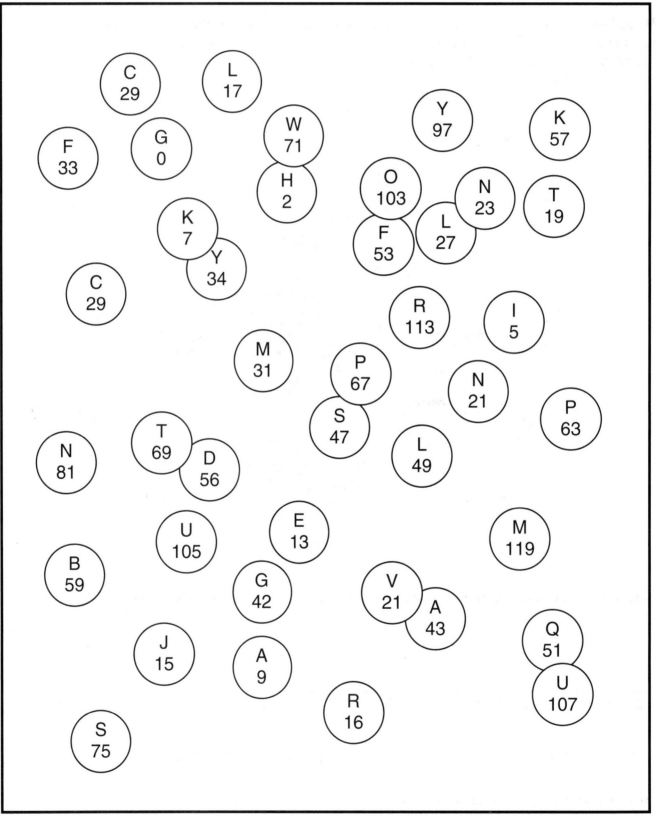

Time for a Treat *(cont.)*

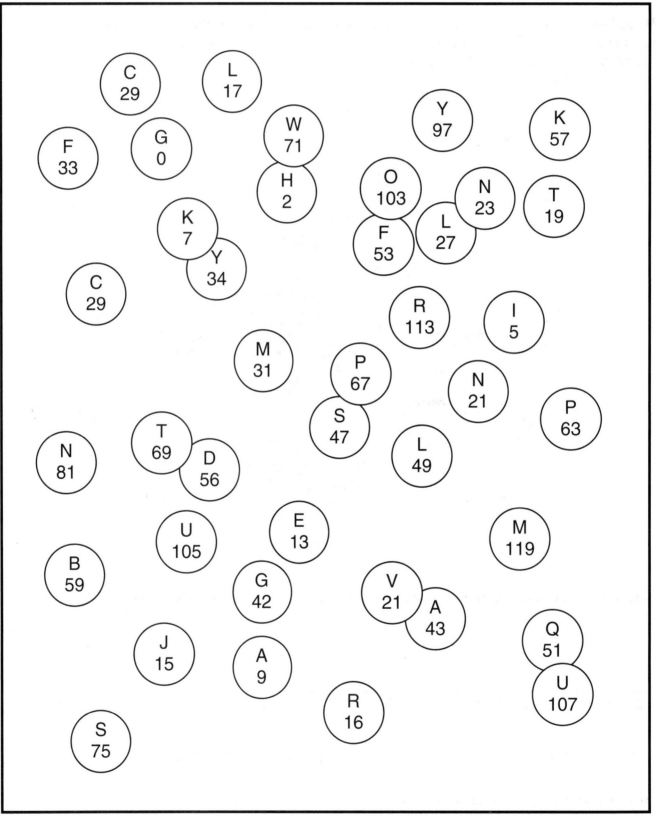

C 29
L 17
Y 97
K 57
F 33
G 0
W 71
H 2
O 103
N 23
T 19
K 7
F 53
L 27
Y 34
C 29
R 113
I 5
M 31
P 67
N 21
S 47
P 63
N 81
T 69
D 56
L 49
U 105
E 13
M 119
B 59
G 42
V 21
A 43
J 15
A 9
Q 51
R 16
U 107
S 75

A Penny for Your Thoughts

Directions: Find the prime factorization for each number surrounding the penny. Then complete the statement below by filling in the blanks. To fill in a blank, look at the prime factorization written below it, and insert the matching letter from the penny.

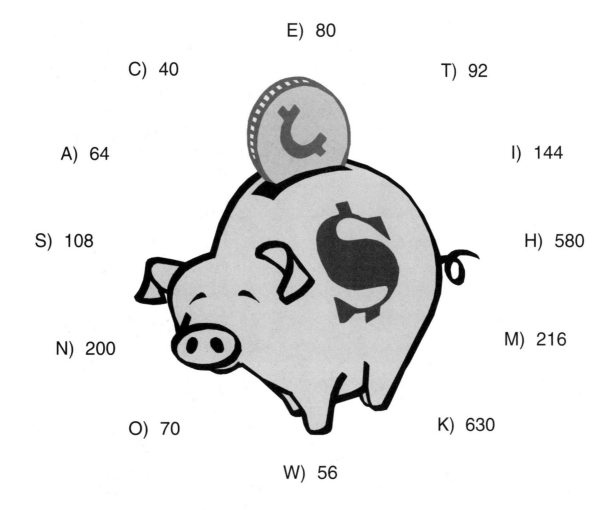

E) 80

C) 40　　　　　　　　　　　　　　　T) 92

A) 64　　　　　　　　　　　　　　　　I) 144

S) 108　　　　　　　　　　　　　　　H) 580

N) 200　　　　　　　　　　　　　　M) 216

O) 70　　　　　　　　　　K) 630

W) 56

Finish the Statement: A man who constantly says, "A penny for your thoughts" . . .

| $2^4 \times 3^2$ | $2^2 \times 3^3$ | | 2^6 | | $2^3 \times 3^3$ | 2^6 | $2^3 \times 5^2$ |

| $2^3 \times 7$ | $2^2 \times 5 \times 29$ | $2 \times 5 \times 7$ | | $2^3 \times 3^3$ | 2^6 | $2 \times 3^2 \times 5 \times 7$ | $2^4 \times 5$ | $2^2 \times 3^3$ |

| $2^3 \times 5^2$ | $2 \times 5 \times 7$ | | $2^3 \times 5$ | $2^4 \times 5$ | $2^3 \times 5^2$ | $2^2 \times 23$ | $2^2 \times 3^3$ |

Focus: Finding the prime factorization of numbers

Surprise Dish

Directions: Complete the factor trees to find the prime factorization for each number. To be sure that you are breaking the numbers down correctly, pay close attention to the clues provided. When you place a correct number in a bubble containing a letter, look at the blank spaces below. Find the number which you placed in the bubble and then write the letter from that bubble on the line. **Note:** Not all shapes have a corresponding letter. Not all letters provided will be used to solve the riddle.

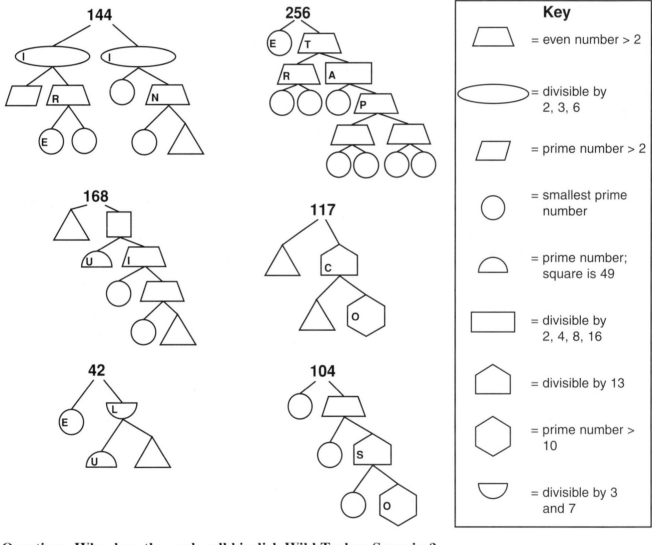

Question: Why does the cook call his dish Wild Turkey Surprise?

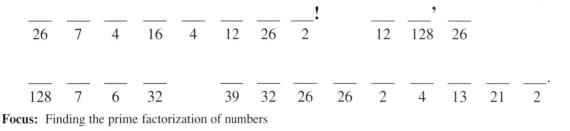

__ __ __ __ __ __ __ __!   __ __ , __
26 7 4 16 4 12 26 2   12 128 26

__ __ __ __   __ __ __ __ __ __ __ __ __ __.
128 7 6 32   39 32 26 26 2 4 13 21 2

Focus: Finding the prime factorization of numbers

From a Lawyer's Lips

Directions: Find the greatest common factor for each set of numbers or monomials. Then look for each answer in the box below, and notice the letter above it. Write the letter in the blank space above the number of the problem.

1. 14, 35, 56

2. 18, 36, 45

3. 3, 5, 7

4. 100, 112

5. $50r, 75r^3, 125r^2$

6. $44r, 48ry$

7. $6mn, 12m^2n, 14mn^2$

8. $-20r, 30r^3$

9. $24b^3, 36bc, 48c$

10. 40, -120, -180

11. $48m^2n^2, 56m^2n$

12. $8a^2r, 12ar, 18r$

13. $114ar, 154a^2br^3$

14. $-18mn, -13mn, 12mn$

A	B	C	D	E	F	G	H	I	J	K	L	M
1	$2ar$	$2mn$	3	$2r$	4	$4ry$	$4r$	mn	7	$7m$	$7ar$	8

N	O	P	Q	R	S	T	U	V	W	X	Y	Z
$8m^2n$	9	$9bc$	$10m$	$10r$	12	20	$25r$	$25ry$	$26m$	45	$48r^2$	$50r$

Question: What does a speedy lawyer say when he emerges from a courtroom or when his wife gives him the same thing every year for Christmas?

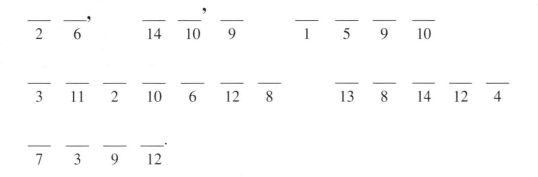

$$\overline{}\ \overline{},\quad \overline{}\ \overline{}'\ \overline{}\qquad \overline{}\ \overline{}\ \overline{}\ \overline{}$$
$$\ \ 2\ \ \ 6\qquad\quad 14\ \ 10\ \ 9\qquad\ 1\ \ \ 5\ \ \ 9\ \ 10$$

$$\overline{}\ \overline{}\ \overline{}\ \overline{}\ \overline{}\ \overline{}\ \overline{}\qquad \overline{}\ \overline{}\ \overline{}\ \overline{}\ \overline{}$$
$$\ \ 3\ \ 11\ \ 2\ \ 10\ \ 6\ \ 12\ \ 8\qquad 13\ \ 8\ \ 14\ \ 12\ \ 4$$

$$\overline{}\ \overline{}\ \overline{}\ \overline{}.$$
$$\ \ 7\ \ \ 3\ \ \ 9\ \ 12$$

Focus: Finding the greatest common factor among monomials

The Bacon Company

Directions: Find the least common multiple for each set of numbers or monomials. Then look for each answer in the box below, and notice the letter above it. Write the letter in the blank space above the number of the problem.

1. 12, 18
2. 6, 9, 15
3. 3, 9, 15
4. 14, 18, 21
5. 4, 10, 22
6. $16x^2y^3z$, $20xy^2z^3$
7. 90, 225, 315

8. $78x^2$, $26y^3$, $104z^3$
9. $4x^2y$, $27xyz^3$
10. $16z^2$, $36x^2y$
11. 8x, 24y, 36z
12. $9x^2y$, $12yz^2$, $15z^2$
13. 4x, 14, $35xy^2$

A	B	C	D	E	F	G	H
36	45	90	112	126	130	186	220

I	J	K	L	M	N	O	P
3150	4000	36xyz	$48x^2y$	72xyz	$80x^2y^3z^3$	$86x^2y^3z^3$	$100x^2yz^3$

Q	R	S	T	U	V	W	X
$105x^2yz^2$	$108x^2yz^3$	$140xy^2$	$144x^2yz^2$	$180x^2yz^2$	$240xy^2$	$312x^2y^3z^3$	$400x^2y^3z^3$

Y	Z
480xyz	560x yz.

Question: Why did the man name his new bacon company after himself?

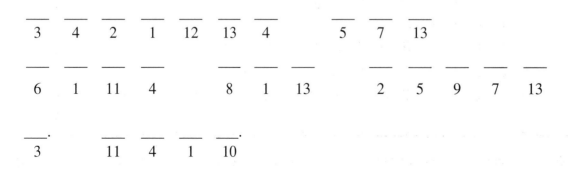

__ __ __ __ __ __ __   __ __ __
3 4 2 1 12 13 4   5 7 13

__ __ __ __   __ __ __   __ __ __ __ __
6 1 11 4   8 1 13   2 5 9 7 13

__.   __ __ __ __.
3   11 4 1 10

Focus: Finding the least common multiple among monomials

Term Search

Directions: Below you will find some mathematical terms which you should be familiar with. Search for the terms in the puzzle and circle them.

Terms

Absolute value	Equivalent	Power
Ascending	Exponent	Prime
Composite	Factorization	Product
Denominator	Integer	Proportion
Descend	Inequality	Quotient
Difference	Inverse	Ratio
Distributive	Multiple	Reciprocal
Dividend	Numerator	Solution
Equation	Opposite	Sum

```
N  O  I  T  A  U  Q  E  F  F  E  U  M  D  O  S  L  T
N  A  B  S  O  L  U  T  E  V  A  L  U  E  T  B  U  E
O  S  E  C  E  N  O  I  T  U  L  O  S  N  I  A  R  V
I  C  R  O  M  T  T  O  R  T  R  E  O  B  E  O  A
T  E  O  M  I  N  I  A  E  Q  S  L  N  M  U  V  T  L
A  N  E  P  R  E  E  R  A  U  A  N  U  I  T  I  A  I
Z  D  N  O  P  N  N  E  T  V  O  L  M  N  N  P  R  N
I  I  E  S  P  O  T  M  I  I  T  I  E  A  O  R  E  E
R  N  N  I  O  P  S  U  U  I  L  Y  R  T  I  O  M  Q
O  G  V  T  W  X  Q  I  P  T  I  P  A  O  T  D  U  U
T  C  T  E  E  E  U  L  T  O  I  T  A  R  R  U  N  A
C  U  B  R  R  G  E  L  R  E  C  I  P  R  O  C  A  L
A  D  N  E  C  S  E  D  A  D  D  V  D  I  P  T  Q  I
F  O  D  I  F  F  E  R  E  N  C  E  V  N  O  M  E  T
U  R  A  C  T  M  D  N  E  D  I  V  I  D  R  O  N  Y
S  P  E  V  I  T  U  B  I  R  T  S  I  D  P  I  I  O
```

(**Teacher Note:** You may wish to have the students look up the definitions and/or make up an example for each word.)

Focus: Familiarizing oneself with common algebraic terms

A "Sharking" Discovery

Directions: Three of the fractions to the right of each problem will be equivalent to the original fraction. Circle the fraction which is NOT equivalent to the original fraction. When you have finished 1–10, the letters above each of the circled fractions will form a sentence that answers the question in the box below. Write the answer sentence in the box.

		BE	AN	IN	IT
1.	**3/6**	1/2	12/24	45/90	54/102
		DH	WA	CA	WI
2.	**4/9**	8/18	16/81	16/36	72/162
		SA	AD	US	LL
3.	**36/48**	18/28	3/4	9/12	72/96
		EI	MA	BE	HA
4.	**9/30**	3/10	36/112	54/180	72/240
		DB	SE	NO	NE
5.	**2/3**	16/24	12/18	46/69	4/9
		TO	AT	TO	AT
6.	**21/51**	7/17	17/68	63/153	42/102
		WI	IN	IN	IN
7.	**$5y^2/8y$**	25y/40	35y/56	$105y^2/168$	125y/200
		TH	TH	GS	ST
8.	**$54ac^2/72a$**	$3c^2/4$	$18c^2/24$	18c/24	$108c^2/144$
		HA	HI	RA	RU
9.	**7jk/15k**	28/60k	21j/45	42jk/90k	56j/120
		RK	RK	RK	RK
10.	**$51m^2/57m$**	17m/10	34m/38	17m/19	153m/171

Question: Why wasn't the girl afraid of the shark?

_____

_____

_____

Focus: Simplifying and identifying equivalent fractions

The Problem with Pachyderms

Directions: Solve each problem. Be sure to reduce your final answer. Look for your answer inside the elephant. There you will find a letter next to each answer. To find the answer to the question below, write the corresponding letter on the blank space(s) provided for each problem.

1. $3\,^2/_3 + 8\,^7/_{12}$

2. $14\,^5/_6 + 5\,^7/_9$

3. $12\,^1/_4 - 9\,^3/_8$

4. $17\,^7/_9 - 12\,^1/_3$

5. $8\,^9/_{10} - 6\,^7/_{10}$

6. $5\,^1/_5 - 2\,^1/_2$

7. $6\,^2/_5 + 1\,^3/_4$

8. $2\,^3/_8 + 3\,^1/_2$

9. $11\,^7/_9 - 2\,^3/_9$

10. $17\,^{11}/_{20} + 13\,^5/_{20}$

11. $8\,^2/_3 - 2\,^1/_4 - 3\,^1/_6$

12. $2\,^1/_5 + 5\,^3/_4 - 1\,^5/_6$

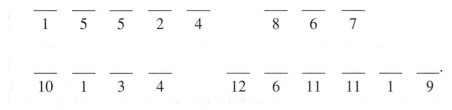

Question: What's the best thing to do if you find an elephant in your bed?

$\overline{}\ \overline{}\ \overline{}\ \overline{}\ \overline{}\quad \overline{}\ \overline{}\ \overline{}$
  1   5   5   2   4   8   6   7

$\overline{}\ \overline{}\ \overline{}\ \overline{}\quad \overline{}\ \overline{}\ \overline{}\ \overline{}\ \overline{}\ \overline{}.$
 10   1   3   4   12   6   11   11   1   9

Focus: Adding and subtracting mixed numbers

"Stair" Crazy

Directions: Solve each equation. Then find the answer under the blank(s) below. Finally, to solve the riddle, write the variable of the equation in the blank.

1. $d + 1.3 = -8.2$ $d =$ _____

2. $n + 23.9 = 25.1$ $n =$ _____

3. $t + 18.4 = 16.7$ $t =$ _____

4. $m - 6.5 = -10$ $m =$ _____

5. $i - 3.6 = 3.4$ $i =$ _____

6. $r + \frac{5}{8} = 2\frac{1}{2}$ $r =$ _____

7. $g + 3\frac{2}{8} = 5$ $g =$ _____

8. $a - \frac{3}{5} = -3\frac{1}{5}$ $a =$ _____

9. $s + -\frac{2}{5} = \frac{1}{3}$ $s =$ _____

10. $f - 4\frac{7}{8} = 6\frac{5}{6}$ $f =$ _____

11. $o - 5.83 = -10.72$ $o =$ _____

12. $u - \frac{1}{9} = -4\frac{4}{6}$ $u =$ _____

13. $e - 2\frac{1}{8} = -4\frac{1}{6}$ $e =$ _____

14. $1 - 2.7 = -11.5$ $1 =$ _____

15. $h + 13.8 = 9.51$ $h =$ _____

Question: What did the boy think when the girl went tumbling down the stairs?

___	___		___	___	___	___	___	___	___
-4.29	$-2\frac{1}{24}$		-1.7	-4.29	-4.89	$-4\frac{5}{9}$	$1\frac{3}{4}$	-4.29	-1.7

___	___	___	___		___	___	___
-1.7	-4.29	$-2\frac{3}{5}$	-1.7		$\frac{11}{15}$	-4.29	$-2\frac{1}{24}$

___	___	___		___	___	___	___	___	___
-4.29	$-2\frac{3}{5}$	-9.5		$11\frac{17}{24}$	$-2\frac{3}{5}$	-8.8	-8.8	$-2\frac{1}{24}$	1.2

___	___	___		___	___	___ .
$11\frac{17}{24}$	-4.89	$1\frac{7}{8}$		-4.29	7	-3.5

Focus: Solving equations involving addition and subtraction of rational numbers (with an emphasis on decimals and fractions)

Rabbit Riddle

Directions: Find the next two terms of each sequence. Then look for the answers on the spaces below. Fill the spaces with the letters for the answers. The resulting words will be the answer to the riddle. (**Note:** Not every answer has a space below.)

1. 8, 16, 24, 32, _____, _____
                     M   N

2. 1, 8, 27, 64, _____, _____
                   A   E

3. 1, 3, 9, 27, _____, _____
                  S   T

4. 1, 4, 7, 10, _____, _____
                 H   I

5. 1, 1, 2, 3, 5, _____, _____
                F   H

6. 7, 4, 1, -2, -5, _____, _____
                   C   D

7. 3, 4.5, 6, 7.5, _____, _____
                 X   Y

8. 6.89, 7, 7.11, 7.22, _____, _____
                      Q   R

9. 1, 3, 7, 13, 21, _____, _____
                  K   L

10. 5, -1, 2, -4, -1, _____, _____
                   G   P

Question: What did the construction worker say when the rabbit stepped onto the forklift?

___ ___ ,   ___ ___ ___ ___   ___ ___
40 10.5   243 13 16 81   16 81

___ ___ ___ ___ ___ ___ ___ ___ ___ ___   ___
-11 216 8 16 48 16 243 216 43 10.5   125

___ ___ ___ ___   —   ___ ___ ___ ___ ___ ___ ___
13 125 7.44 216   7.44 125 16 81 16 48 -7

___ ___ ___ ___ ___ ___ ___ ___ ___ ___ !
216 9 -4 216 7.44 16 216 48 -8 216

Focus: Completing mathematical sequences

Pilot Puzzle

Directions: Solve each multiplication problem, and then complete the puzzle. After filling in the puzzle, you will notice that some blocks have letters in them. To learn the answer to the riddle, use the number that you wrote in the block containing the letter and the direction (across or down) of the problem, and write the letter in the appropriate blank space below.

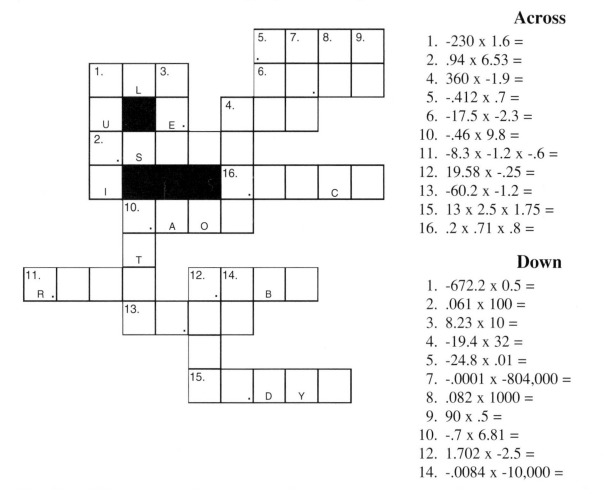

Across

1. -230 x 1.6 =
2. .94 x 6.53 =
4. 360 x -1.9 =
5. -.412 x .7 =
6. -17.5 x -2.3 =
10. -.46 x 9.8 =
11. -8.3 x -1.2 x -.6 =
12. 19.58 x -.25 =
13. -60.2 x -1.2 =
15. 13 x 2.5 x 1.75 =
16. .2 x .71 x .8 =

Down

1. -672.2 x 0.5 =
2. .061 x 100 =
3. 8.23 x 10 =
4. -19.4 x 32 =
5. -24.8 x .01 =
7. -.0001 x -804,000 =
8. .082 x 1000 =
9. 90 x .5 =
10. -.7 x 6.81 =
12. 1.702 x -2.5 =
14. -.0084 x -10,000 =

Question: What do you call a pilot who flies across the country twice and never has time to take a shower?

$$\overline{}$$
5 →

$$\overline{} \quad \overline{} \quad \overline{} \quad \overline{} \quad \overline{} \qquad \overline{} \quad \overline{} \quad \overline{} \quad \overline{} \quad \overline{} \quad \overline{} \qquad \overline{}$$
8 →   1↓   -5 →   7↓   7 →   8 →   0 →   3↓   9 →   6 →   2↓

$$\overline{} \quad \overline{} \quad \overline{} \quad \overline{} \quad \overline{} \quad \overline{} \quad \overline{}!$$
3 →   -5 →   0 →   1 →   1 →   2↓   -5 →

Focus: Multiplying positive and negative decimals

Duck Cookies

Directions: Below you will find the ingredients in a recipe for duck cookies. You must determine if each ingredient in the recipe is doubled, tripled, halved, or cut into thirds. For example, look at number one. Make four calculations. What would $\frac{1}{2}$ jar be if it were doubled, tripled, halved, and cut into thirds? The only possible answer would be A because a $\frac{1}{2}$ jar of pickles, when doubled, would be 1 jar. There is only one correct answer per line. Circle the correct amount, and notice the letter next to the answer. Write that letter on the empty space above with the number of the problem you just solved. The resulting message will be the answer to the riddle.

Duck Cookies	Double	Triple	Cut in Half	Cut into Thirds
1. $\frac{1}{2}$ jar pickles	A. 1 jar	B. $\frac{1}{6}$ jar	C. 1 jar	D. $\frac{3}{2}$ jar
2. 2 sardines	B. 1 sardine	C. $\frac{2}{3}$ sardine	B. 1 sardine	C. 6 sardines
3. $\frac{3}{4}$ cup sugar	N. $\frac{3}{8}$ cup	M. $\frac{3}{12}$ cup	R. $\frac{3}{8}$ cup	S. $\frac{9}{4}$ cup
4. $\frac{1}{3}$ tsp. honey	A. $\frac{1}{6}$ tsp.	E. 1 tsp.	I. $\frac{2}{3}$ tsp.	O. $\frac{2}{9}$ tbsp.
5. 45 raisins	A. 92 raisins	E. 150 raisins	I. 28.5 raisins	O. 15 raisins
6. $\frac{2}{3}$ cup sour milk	S. 1 $\frac{1}{3}$ cup	T. 2 $\frac{1}{3}$ cup	U. $\frac{1}{6}$ cup	R. 2 cups
7. $\frac{1}{3}$ bag brown sugar	S. $\frac{1}{6}$ bag	T. $\frac{1}{9}$ bag	U. $\frac{1}{6}$ bag	R. 1 bag
8. $\frac{1}{4}$ tbsp. vanilla	L. $\frac{1}{8}$ tbsp.	M. $\frac{1}{12}$ tbsp.	N. $\frac{1}{6}$ tsp.	O. $\frac{1}{12}$ tbsp.
9. $\frac{2}{3}$ cup bread crumbs	A. $\frac{2}{6}$ cup	B. $\frac{2}{9}$ cup	C. $\frac{1}{3}$ cup	D. $\frac{2}{11}$ cup
10. $\frac{1}{5}$ bag flour	E. $\frac{1}{10}$ bag	F. $\frac{3}{5}$ bag	G. $\frac{2}{5}$ bag	H. $\frac{3}{5}$ bag
11. 3 pieces of celery	K. 6 pieces	L. 1 piece	M. 6 pieces	N. $\frac{3}{4}$ piece
12. 14 candies	W. 29 candies	X. 42 candies	Y. 8 candies	Z. 4 $\frac{1}{3}$ candies
13. $\frac{1}{3}$ cup carrot	Q. $\frac{2}{3}$ cup	R. $\frac{1}{9}$ cup	S. $\frac{2}{3}$ cup	T. 1 cup

Question: What did the duck eat for lunch?

$\overline{}$ $\overline{}$ $\overline{}$ $\overline{}$ $\overline{}$ $\overline{}$
1 2 8 12 5 10

$\overline{}$ $\overline{}$ $\overline{}$ $\overline{}$ $\overline{}$ $\overline{}$ $\overline{}$ $\overline{}$
13 7 1 9 11 4 3 6

Focus: Multiplying and dividing fractions

A Dating Disaster

Directions: Solve each equation in the heart. After solving each equation, notice the letter above it. Then match the letter with the answer on the space(s) below. The resulting message will be the answer to the riddle.

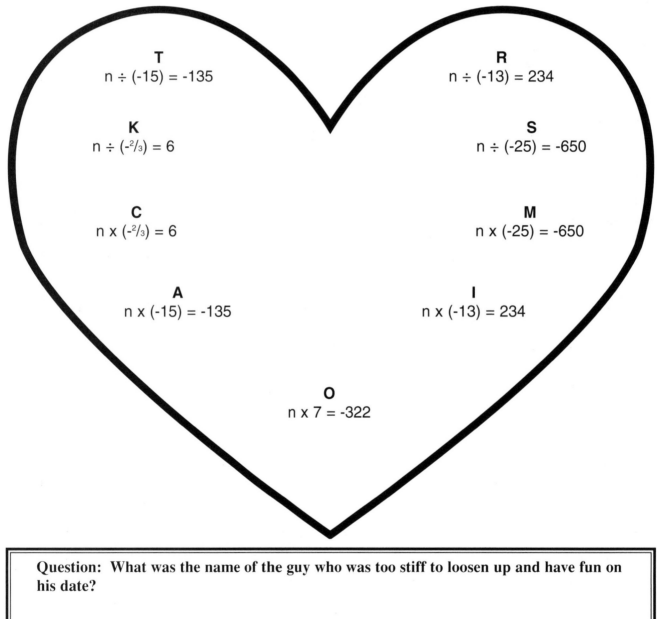

T
n ÷ (-15) = -135

R
n ÷ (-13) = 234

K
n ÷ (-²/₃) = 6

S
n ÷ (-25) = -650

C
n x (-²/₃) = 6

M
n x (-25) = -650

A
n x (-15) = -135

I
n x (-13) = 234

O
n x 7 = -322

Question: What was the name of the guy who was too stiff to loosen up and have fun on his date?

_____	_____	_____	_____		_____.
-3042	-18	-9	-4		9

_____	_____	_____	_____	_____	_____
26	-46	-3042	2025	-18	16,250

Focus: Solving multiplication and division equations

Reggae Frog

Directions: Write each of the following numbers in scientific notation. Then, using the exponent from the answer, look at the "Exponents" column for the letter which coincides with the exponent. Write this letter in the blank which matches the problem number. The resulting message will be an answer to the riddle.

Number	Scientific Notation	Exponents
1. 108,000,000	_____	9 = B -1 = R
2. -1,080,000,000	_____	
3. 5000	_____	8 = D -2 = A
4. .00053	_____	
5. 580	_____	7 = E -3 = Y
6. .0000278	_____	
7. -.00400067	_____	6 = H -4 = P
8. 930,000	_____	
9. -52,480	_____	5 = N -5 = R
10. 56,300,000	_____	
11. .0000065	_____	4 = O -6 = P
12. 49	_____	
13. .73	_____	3 = O -7 = Y
14. 6,700,400	_____	
15. -.000000785	_____	2 = T -8 = S
		1 = W -9 = L

Question: What might a frog who loves reggae music say to his pal who is feeling down?

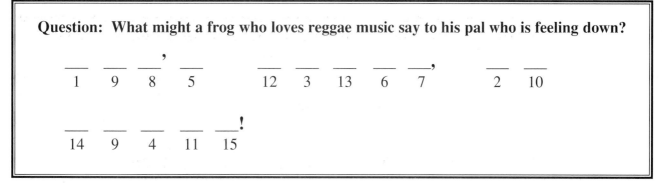

___ ___ ___ , ___   ___ ___ ___ ___ ___ ,   ___ ___
  1   9   8   5   12   3   13   6   7   2   10

___ ___ ___ ___ ___ !
 14   9   4   11   15

Focus: Writing numbers in scientific notation

Words of Wisdom

Directions: Solve each two-step equation. Find each answer in the answer column on the right and notice the letter next to it. Write that letter in the blank space above the number of the problem at the bottom of the page.

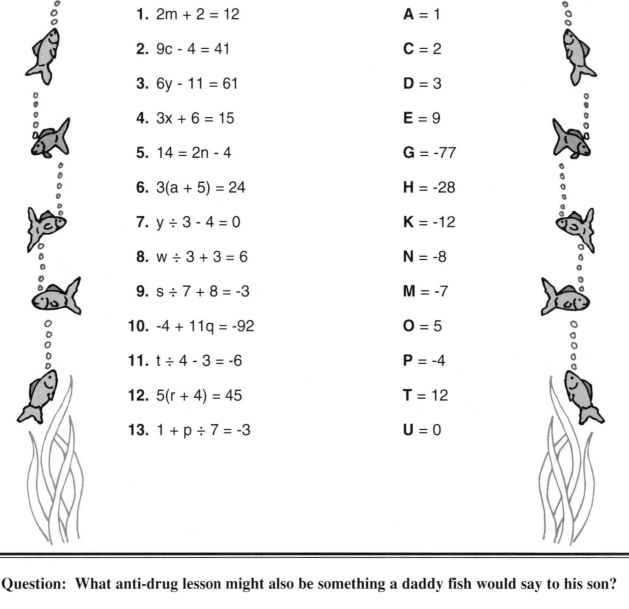

1. $2m + 2 = 12$

2. $9c - 4 = 41$

3. $6y - 11 = 61$

4. $3x + 6 = 15$

5. $14 = 2n - 4$

6. $3(a + 5) = 24$

7. $y \div 3 - 4 = 0$

8. $w \div 3 + 3 = 6$

9. $s \div 7 + 8 = -3$

10. $-4 + 11q = -92$

11. $t \div 4 - 3 = -6$

12. $5(r + 4) = 45$

13. $1 + p \div 7 = -3$

A = 1

C = 2

D = 3

E = 9

G = -77

H = -28

K = -12

N = -8

M = -7

O = 5

P = -4

T = 12

U = 0

Question: What anti-drug lesson might also be something a daddy fish would say to his son?

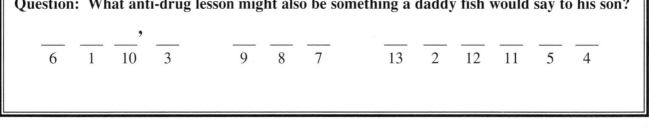

____ ____ ____ , ____   ____ ____ ____   ____ ____ ____ ____ ____ ____
 6   1   10   3   9   8   7   13   2   12   11   5   4

Focus: Solving two-step equations

Go, Team, Go!

Directions: Solve each equation. Read the question in the box below. To find the answer, write the variable from each problem on the blank space that contains the correct answer.

1. $6r - 3 = 9r - 6$

2. $7n + 5 = 8n + 10$

3. $3b + 18 = 2b + 12$

4. $3e + 6 = 2e + 5$

5. $\dfrac{a + 2}{5} = -2 + a$

6. $4u - 4 = -10u + 24$

7. $3a + 2 = 11$

8. $-c \div 3 - 5 = -17$

9. $-k + (-7) = 3k + 1$

10. $-s + 2 = -3s - 6$

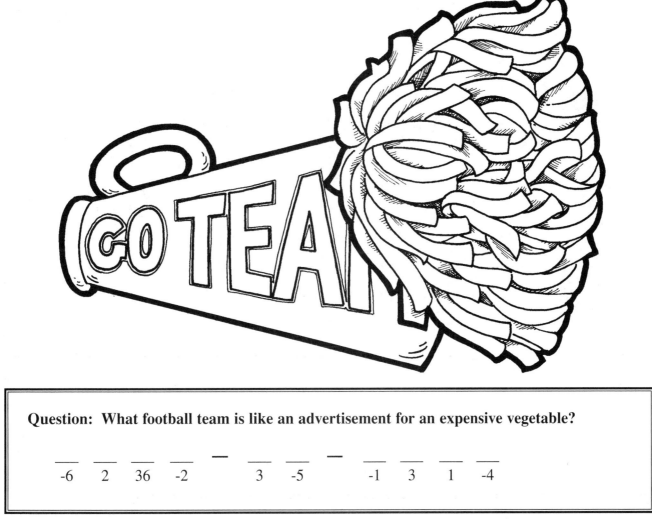

Question: What football team is like an advertisement for an expensive vegetable?

$\overline{}$ $\overline{}$ $\overline{}$ $\overline{}$ $\quad$ $\overline{}$ $\overline{}$ $\quad$ $\overline{}$ $\overline{}$ $\overline{}$ $\overline{}$

$\;$ -6 $\quad$ 2 $\quad$ 36 $\quad$ -2 $\qquad$ 3 $\quad$ -5 $\qquad$ -1 $\quad$ 3 $\quad$ 1 $\quad$ -4

Focus: Solving equations with variables on both sides of the equal sign

Baby Genius

Directions: Solve each multi-step equation. Find each answer in the answer column on the right and notice the letter next to it. Write that letter in the blank space above the number of the problem at the bottom of the page.

1. $4(n + 3) = 28$

2. $2(t - 3) = 10$

3. $3 = (x \div 9) - 2$

4. $6b + 9 = -4b + 29$

5. $-8 + 4m = m - 23$

6. $\dfrac{(x + 8)}{-3} = 6$

7. $4(x - 2) = 9(x + 3)$

8. $3(r + 1) = 5(r - 3) + 8$

9. $13y + 11 = -5(y - 7)$

10. $-6(x - 2) = 18$

11. $-2(a + 3) = 12 + 4a$

12. $-j - 2(j + 9) = 0$

13. $(3x + 5) + 31 = -6(2x - 1)$

14. $6y - 2(y - 8) = 0$

15. $-7(c - 9) = 0$

16. $3(p - 3) = 4p - 1$

Answers

A = -26
B = -8
C = -7
D = -6
E = -5
G = -4
H = -3
I = -2
L = -1
N = 1 1/3
O = 2
P = 4
S = 5
T = 8
U = 9
Y = 45

Question: Why did the mother think that her baby was a mathematical genius after their parrot died?

$\overline{}\ \overline{}\ \overline{}\ \overline{}\ \overline{}\ \overline{}\ \overline{}\qquad \overline{}\ \overline{}\ \overline{}$
16   5   7   6   15   8   5   2   11   5

$\overline{}\ \overline{}\ \overline{}\ \overline{}\qquad \overline{}\ \overline{}\ \overline{}\ \overline{}$,
16   6   16   3   8   6   13   12

"$\overline{}\ \overline{}\ \overline{}\ \overline{}\ \overline{}\ \overline{}\ \overline{}$!"
1   4   10   3   14   4   9

Focus: Solving multi-step equations

You Are What You Drink

Directions: There are two correct answers for each solution that is graphed. Write the variable of the equation or inequality that is INCORRECT on the blank space which corresponds to each problem. The resulting words will give you the answer to the riddle.

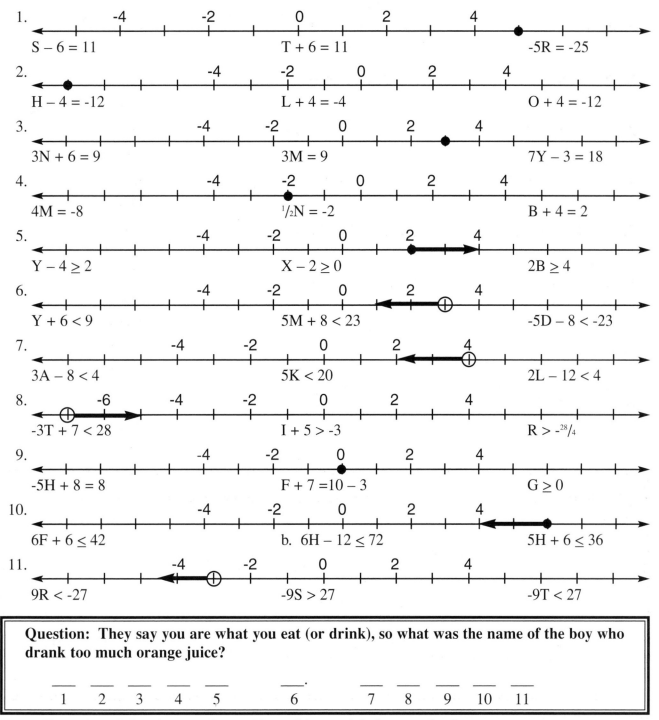

1. $S - 6 = 11$ $T + 6 = 11$ $-5R = -25$

2. $H - 4 = -12$ $L + 4 = -4$ $O + 4 = -12$

3. $3N + 6 = 9$ $3M = 9$ $7Y - 3 = 18$

4. $4M = -8$ $\frac{1}{2}N = -2$ $B + 4 = 2$

5. $Y - 4 \geq 2$ $X - 2 \geq 0$ $2B \geq 4$

6. $Y + 6 < 9$ $5M + 8 < 23$ $-5D - 8 < -23$

7. $3A - 8 < 4$ $5K < 20$ $2L - 12 < 4$

8. $-3T + 7 < 28$ $I + 5 > -3$ $R > -{}^{28}/_4$

9. $-5H + 8 = 8$ $F + 7 = 10 - 3$ $G \geq 0$

10. $6F + 6 \leq 42$ b. $6H - 12 \leq 72$ $5H + 6 \leq 36$

11. $9R < -27$ $-9S > 27$ $-9T < 27$

Question: They say you are what you eat (or drink), so what was the name of the boy who drank too much orange juice?

___ ___ ___ ___ ___   ___ .   ___ ___ ___ ___ ___
 1   2   3   4   5   6   7   8   9 10 11

Focus: Comparing solutions from equations and inequalities as graphed on a number line

Write Your Own Riddle

Directions: Use the following coordinate system to match each ordered pair with the letter graphed on that point. On the lines below, write the letter above each ordered pair to write a riddle question as well as to answer it.

Riddle Question

___	___	___		___	___	___			
(-3,-11)	(7,3)	(3,-6)		(0,-9)	(6,-4)	(0,-9)			

___	___	___		___	___	___	___	___	___
(4,5)	(7,3)	(-9,0)		(-5,5)	(-7,4)	(1,-1)	(0,9)	(-9,0)	(1,-1)

___	___	___	___		___	___	___	___	___
(0,-9)	(-7,4)	(0,-9)	(-9,0)		(-2,2)	(1,-1)	(-6,-2)	(-5,5)	(-5,5)

___	___	___		___	___	___	___	___	?
(4,5)	(7,3)	(-9,0)		(-6,-2)	(-2,2)	(-9,0)	(1,1)	(-10,-9)	

Answer:

___	___		___	___	___		___	___
(4,5)	(-6,-2)		(9,0)	(-9,0)	(4,5)		(4,5)	(-6,-2)

___	___	___		___	___	___	___	___
(4,5)	(7,3)	(-9,0)		(-6,-2)	(4,5)	(7,3)	(-9,0)	(1,-1)

___	___	___	___
(4,5)	(6,-4)	(0,-9)	(-9,0)

Focus: Finding coordinates in the Cartesian Coordinate System

Smile!

Directions: Graph each of the points on this and the next page on graph paper (see page 44 for graph paper). Connect the points as you go. When you read the words, "New Line Segment," stop and start a new line. You should have a picture when you are finished.

Start
1. (-6.5, 9.5)
2. (-6, 10)
3. (-5.5, 11)
4. (-4.5, 11)
5. (-3, 10.5)
6. (-2, 9.5)
7. (-1.5, 8)
8. (-1.5, 7)
9. (-1.5, 6)
10. (-1.5, 5)
11. (-2, 4)
12. (-3, 3)
13. (-3.5, 2.5)
14. (-4, 2)
15. (-5, 2)
16. (-6, 2.5)
17. (-6.5, 3)
18. (-7, 3.5)
19. (-7.5, 4.5)
20. (-7.5, 6)
21. (-7.5, 7)
22. (-7, 8)

New Line Segment
23. (-2, 10)
24. (-1, 11)
25. (1, 11)
26. (2.5, 10.5)
27. (3.5, 9.5)
28. (4, 9)
29. (4.5, 8)
30. (4.5, 5)
31. (4, 4)
32. (3, 3)
33. (2, 2.5)
34. (1, 2.5)
35. (0, 2.5)
36. (-1, 3)
37. (-2, 4)

New Line Segment
38. (-5, 6)
39. (-4, 7)
40. (-3, 6)
41. (-4, 5)

New Line Segment
42. (1, 6)
43. (2, 7)
44. (3, 6)
45. (2, 5)

New Line Segment
46. (-7, 12)
47. (-4, 12)
48. (-5, 13)
49. (-6, 13)
50. (-7, 12)

New Line Segment
51. (-2, 12)
52. (2, 12)
53. (1, 13)
54. (-1, 13)
55. (-2, 12)

New Line Segment
56. (-11, 8)
57. (-12, 7.5)
58. (-13, 7)
59. (-13.5, 6)
60. (-13.5, 3)
61. (-12.5, 2)
62. (-12.5, 1)
63. (-12, 0)
64. (-11, -0.5)
65. (-10, -0.5)
66. (-9.5, 0)

New Line Segment
67. (6.5, 7)
68. (8, 7.5)
69. (9, 6.5)
70. (10, 5.5)
71. (10.5, 4.5)
72. (10.5, 2)
73. (10, 1.5)
74. (9, 1)
75. (8.5, 0.5)
76. (8, -0.5)
77. (7, -0.5)
78. (6.5, 0)

New Line Segment
79. (7, 5)
80. (8, 5.5)
81. (9, 5)
82. (8, 3)

New Line Segment
83. (-10, 5.5)
84. (-11, 6)
85. (-12, 5.5)
86. (-12.5, 5)
87. (-12, 4.5)
88. (-11.5, 3.5)

New Line Segment
89. (-3, 3)
90. (-3, 2)
91. (-3.5, 1)
92. (-4, 0)
93. (-4.5, -1)
94. (-5, -2)
95. (-5, -3)
96. (-4.5, -4)
97. (-3.5, -4.5)
98. (-2.5, -5)
99. (-1.5, -5)
100. (-0.5, -4)

Smile! *(cont.)*

New Line Segment
101. (-10, 0.5)
102. (-10, -0.5)
103. (-9.5, -7)
104. (-9, -9)
105. (-7, -11.5)
106. (-6, -12)
107. (-4, -13.5)
108. (-2, -14)
109. (1, -14)
110. (3, -13)
111. (5, -10)
112. (5.5, -7)
113. (6, -3)
114. (6, 0)

New Line Segment
115. (-8, -3)
116. (-8, -6)
117. (-7.5, -8)
118. (-7, -9)
119. (-6, -10)
120. (-5, -11)
121. (-3, -12.5)
122. (-1, -12.5)
123. (0, -12.5)
124. (1, -12)
125. (2, -11)
126. (3, -10)
127. (3, -3)
128. (2, -5)
129. (1, -5.5)
130. (-1, -6.5)
131. (-3, -6.5)
132. (-4, -6.5)
133. (-5, -6)
134. (-7, -4)
135. (-8, -3)
136. (-7, -7)
137. (-5, -9)

138. (0, -9)
139. (2, -7)
140. (3, -3)
New Line Segment
141. (-7, -4)
142. (-7, -9)
New Line Segment
143. (-5, -6)
144. (-5, -11)
New Line Segment
145. (-3, -6.5)
146. (-3, -12.5)
New Line Segment
147. (-1, -6.5)
148. (-1, -12.5)
New Line Segment
149. (1, -5.5)
150. (1, -12)
New Line Segment
151. (2, -5)
152. (2, -11)
New Line Segment
153. (-10.5, 8)
154. (-11, 9)
155. (-11.5, 8)
156. (-12, 9)
157. (-12.5, 8)
158. (-13.5, 13)
159. (-13, 15)
160. (-14.5, 16.5)
161. (-15.5, 16)
162. (-15, 17)
163. (-14, 17)
164. (-12, 16)
165. (-11, 17)
166. (7, 17)
167. (10.5, 13)

168. (10, 12)
169. (10, 13)
170. (9.5, 12)
171. (9, 13)
172. (8.5, 12)
173. (8, 13)
174. (7.5, 12)
175. (5, 15)
176. (-8, 15)
177. (-10, 13)
178. (-10, 9)
179. (-10.5, 8)
New Line Segment
180. (8, 12)
181. (8, 7.5)
New Line Segment
182. (10, 12)
183. (10, 7)
184. (9, 7)
You're done!

Focus: Graphing coordinates in the Cartesian Coordinate System

You Can Lead Them to Water . . .

Directions: Graph each of the points on the graph paper on page 44. Connect the points as you go. You should have a picture when you are finished.

1. (-5.5, 17)
2. (-5, 16)
3. (-4.5, 15.5)
4. (-6, 12)
5. (-9, 9)
6. (-8.5, 8.5)
7. (-8, 8)
8. (-7, 8.5)
9. (-6.5, 8.5)
10. (-7, 8.5)
11. (-8, 8)
12. (-7, 7)
13. (-6, 7.5)
14. (-6, 8)
15. (-5, 8.5)
16. (-4, 9)
17. (-3, 10)
18. (-4, 10)
19. (-4.5, 10.5)
20. (-4, 10)
21. (-3, 10)
22. (-2, 10.5)
23. (-1.5, 12)
24. (-2, 10.5)
25. (-3, 10)
26. (-2, 9)

27. (-2, 8)
28. (-2, 6)
29. (-1.5, 5)
30. (-1, 3.5)
31. (-3, 3)
32. (-7, 3.5)
33. (-11, 0)
34. (-11, -3)
35. (-9, -3)
36. (-9, -2)
37. (-11, -2)
38. (-9, -2)
39. (-9, -1)
40. (-7.5, 0)
41. (-6, 2)
42. (-7.5, 0)
43. (-9, -2)
44. (-8, -5)
45. (-6, -6)
46. (-5.5, -5)
47. (-5.5, -4)
48. (-6.5, -3)
49. (-7, -3)
50. (-4, 0)
51. (2, 0)
52. (0, 0)

53. (0, -1)
54. (5.5, -7.5)
55. (5.5, -4.5)
56. (5.5, -7.5)
57. (6, -10)
58. (7, -12)
59. (1, -16)
60. (0, -18.5)
61. (1, -19)
62. (2, -19)
63. (3, -18.5)
64. (3.5, -17.5)
65. (3, -17)
66. (9, -15)
67. (11, -12)
68. (13.5, -8)
69. (13.5, -10)
70. (13, -11)
71. (12.5, -12)
72. (12, -13)
73. (11.5, -14)
74. (11, -16)
75. (11, -20)
76. (13, -21)
77. (13, -20.5)
78. (15, -21)

79. (15, -20.5)
80. (16, -21)
81. (14.5, -19)
82. (15, -17)
83. (15, -14.5)
84. (15.5, -12)
85. (15.5, -9)
86. (15, -7)
87. (14, -5)
88. (12, -3)
89. (10, 0)
90. (9, 2)
91. (8, 4)
92. (7.5, 6)
93. (7, 8.5)
94. (9.5, 7)
95. (8, 10.5)
96. (9, 10.5)
97. (7, 15)
98. (9, 16)
99. (3, 18)
100. (4, 20)
101. (0, 18)
102. (-4, 16)
103. (-5.5, 17)

Focus: Graphing coordinates in the Cartesian Coordinate System

Graph Paper (I)

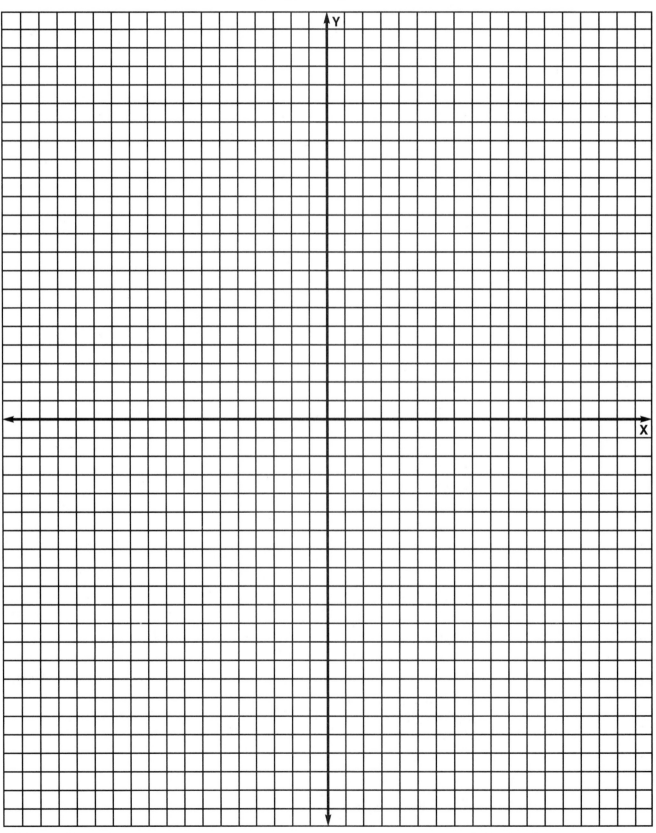

Largest Migrating Mammal

Directions: Graph each of the points on the graph paper on page 46. Connect the points as you go. When you read the words, "New Line Segment," stop and start a new line. You should have a picture when you are finished.

Start
1. (4, 5)
2. (8, 5)
3. (10, 4.5)
4. (13, 3.5)
5. (16, 2)
6. (17, 1)
7. (18, -1)
8. (17, -3)
9. (15, -3.5)
10. (12, -4.5)
11. (11, -4.5)
12. (9, -5)
13. (6, -5)

New Line Segment
14. (18, -1)
15. (10, -1)
16. (9, -1.5)
17. (7.5, -2)
18. (6, -5)
19. (5, -7)
20. (4, -8.5)
21. (2, -10)
22. (1, -10)
23. (-1, -10)
24. (-0.5, -9)
25. (0, -8)
26. (0.5, -7)
27. (1, -5)
28. (1.5, -4)
29. (1.5, -2)

New Line Segment
30. (1, -5)
31. (-1, -5)
32. (-5, -5)
33. (-6, -5)

34. (-9, -4.5)
35. (-10, -4)
36. (-12.5, -2.5)
37. (-14, -4.5)
38. (-16, -5.5)
39. (-18, -6)
40. (-19.5, -7)
41. (-20.5, -7)
42. (-20.5, -6)
43. (-19, -3.5)
44. (-17, -2)
45. (-15, -1)
46. (-16, 0.5)
47. (-18, 1)
48. (-19.5, 3)
49. (-20, 5.5)
50. (-20.5, 6.5)
51. (-19, 5.5)
52. (-15.5, 4)
53. (-14, 2.5)
54. (-12.5, 1)
55. (-11, 2)
56. (-7, 4)
57. (-4, 4.5)
58. (-1, 5)
59. (-2, 8)
60. (-3.5, 12.5)
61. (-2, 12.5)
62. (0, 11.5)
63. (1.5, 10)
64. (2.5, 8)
65. (4, 5)

New Line Segment
66. (-1, -5)
67. (-2.5, -8)
68. (-3, -9)

69. (-0.5, -9)
70. (1.5, -4)
71. (-1, -3.5)
72. (-4.5, -3.5)
73. (-7.5, -4)
74. (-10, -4)

New Line Segment
75. (7.5, 3)
76. (8, 3)
77. (9, 3)
78. (10, 3)
79. (10.5, 2.5)
80. (10.5, 2)
81. (10, 1.5)
82. (9, 1.5)
83. (8, 1.5)
84. (7, 2)

New Line Segment
85. (4.5, 5)
86. (4, 4.5)
87. (4, 4)
88. (7, 4)
89. (7, 4.5)
90. (6.5, 5)

New Line Segment
91. (5.5, 5.5)
92. (5, 6)
93. (5, 6.5)
94. (5.5, 6.5)
95. (5.5, 5.5)

New Line Segment
96. (6, 5.5)
97. (6, 6.5)
98. (6.5, 6.5)
99. (6.5, 6)
100. (6, 5.5)

New Line Segment
101. (5.5, 7)
102. (5, 7.5)
103. (5, 8)
104. (5.5, 8)
105. (5.5, 7)

New Line Segment
106. (5.5, 9)
107. (5, 10)
108. (5.5, 10.5)
109. (6, 10)
110. (5.5, 9)

New Line Segment
111. (7, 7.5)
112. (7, 8.5)
113. (8, 9)
114. (8, 8)
115. (7, 7.5)

New Line Segment
116. (6, 8)
117. (6, 9)
118. (6.5, 9.5)
119. (7, 9)
120. (6, 8)

New Line Segment
121. (5, 8.5)
122. (4, 9)
123. (4, 9.5)
124. (4.5, 9.5)
125. (5, 8.5)

A Single Large Point!
126. (9,1)
You're Done!

Focus: Graphing coordinates in the Cartesian Coordinate System

Graph Paper (II)

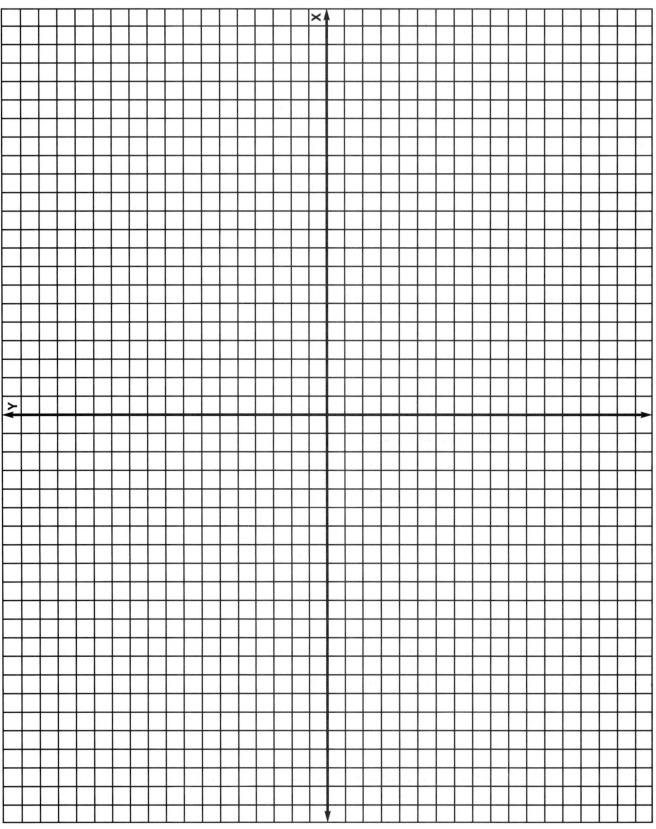

Crisscross

Directions: Graph each equation. Each line will have 2 endpoint letters that are used in the riddle below. Write the first letter (the highest letter on that line) on the first blank of the problem and the second letter on the next blank. The resulting message will be the answer to the riddle.

$\boxed{1, 2}$ $y = x + 2$

$\boxed{3, 4}$ $x + y = 2$

$\boxed{5, 6}$ $y = -3x + 1$

$\boxed{7, 8}$ $y = x - 7$

$\boxed{9, 10}$ $x = -8$

$\boxed{11, 12}$ $y = -2x - 3$

$\boxed{13, 14}$ $x = -5$

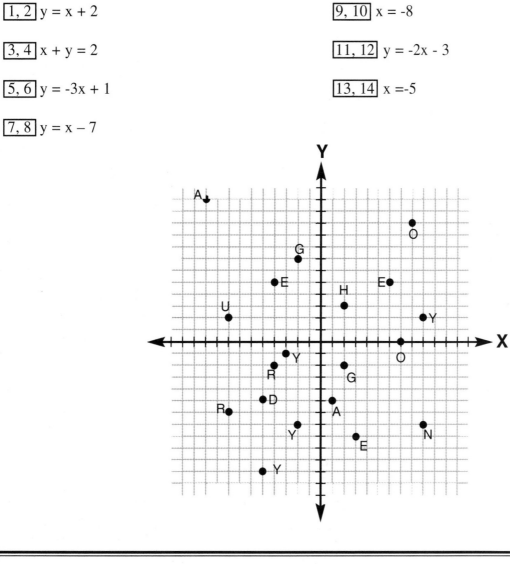

Question: What did the juicer say to the citrus fruit?

___ ___ ___ ___ ___ ___   ___ ___ ___   ___ ___ ___ ___ ___?

1   2   3   4   5   6   7   8   9   10 11 12 13 14

Focus: Graphing linear equations

A Canine Question

Directions: Solve each system of equations below and on page 49 by graphing them. Using the solution, find the letter in the chart on page 49 which matches the solution for each problem. Write this letter on the blank space which is labeled with the problem number. The resulting message will be the answer to the riddle.

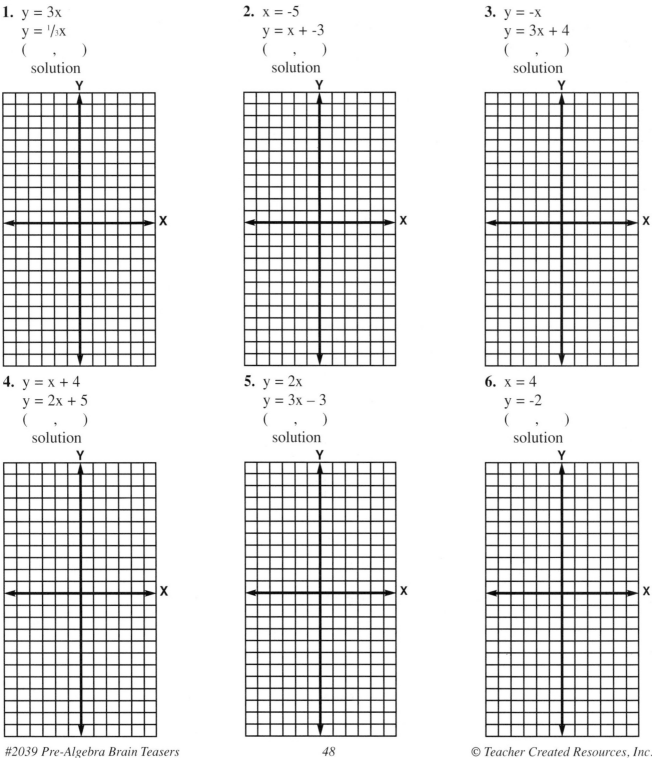

1. $y = 3x$
$y = \frac{1}{3}x$
(,)
solution

2. $x = -5$
$y = x + -3$
(,)
solution

3. $y = -x$
$y = 3x + 4$
(,)
solution

4. $y = x + 4$
$y = 2x + 5$
(,)
solution

5. $y = 2x$
$y = 3x - 3$
(,)
solution

6. $x = 4$
$y = -2$
(,)
solution

A Canine Question *(cont.)*

7. y = 4 + 2x
   y − x = 4
   (,   )
   solution

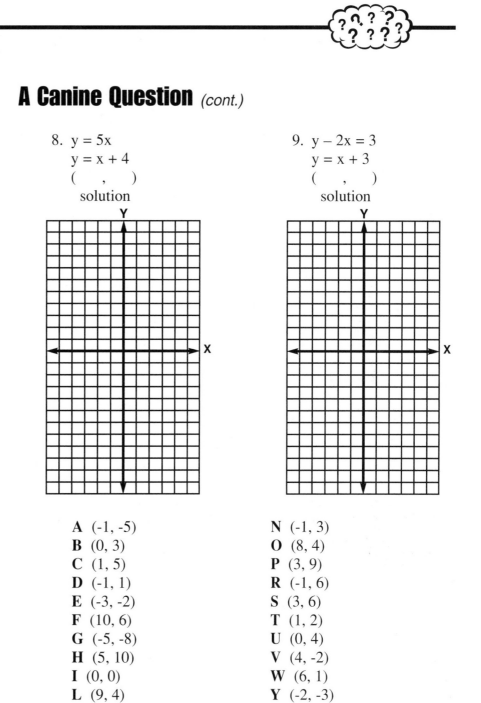

8. y = 5x
   y = x + 4
   (,   )
   solution

9. y − 2x = 3
   y = x + 3
   (,   )
   solution

10. y − 2x = 1
    y − x = -1
    (,   )
    solution

A (-1, -5)
B (0, 3)
C (1, 5)
D (-1, 1)
E (-3, -2)
F (10, 6)
G (-5, -8)
H (5, 10)
I (0, 0)
L (9, 4)
M (-4, -9)

N (-1, 3)
O (8, 4)
P (3, 9)
R (-1, 6)
S (3, 6)
T (1, 2)
U (0, 4)
V (4, -2)
W (6, 1)
Y (-2, -3)

Question: What is it called when a cartoon dog plunges into the water?

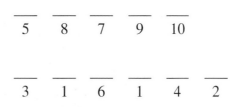

 ___   ___   ___   ___   ___
  5   8   7   9   10

 ___   ___   ___   ___   ___   ___
  3   1   6   1   4   2

Focus: Solving systems of equations by graphing linear equations

A Crossword Puzzle of Graphing Terms

Directions: Find the most appropriate word answer for each item. Then write the word in the blank spaces in the crossword puzzle on page 51.

Across

1. The point on the coordinate plane where the ordered pair is (0, 0).

3. The steepness of a line, measured by the difference of y, divided by the difference of x.

4. The coordinate system is divided into four _____ by the boundary lines of the x and y axes.

6. The x value of the point where a graph crosses the x axis.

9. What is formed by the equation y = mx + b?

10. _____ of equations is the set of equations graphed on the same grid.

11. If all points are on the same line, they are said to be _____.

Down

2. A diagram which shows the relationship between two or more entities.

3. Another name for the answer.

4. What "b" stands for when y = mx + b.

5. When a/an _____ is graphed, we shade above or below the dashed or solid line.

6. The horizontal axis.

7. The plural of axis.

8. _____ are used to locate and graph points in the Cartesian Coordinate System.

Focus: Reviewing terminology associated with graphing

A Crossword Puzzle of Graphing Terms *(cont.)*

Directions: See page 50 for clues.

A Funny Feline

Directions: Use the letters in the word **RATIO** to write a fraction for each ratio. For example, if the item says "the number of Ts : vowels," the ratio would be 1:3 because there are one T and three vowels in the word "ratio." Then look in the fraction box on the right, and notice the letter next to the fraction. Write this letter on the blank space below that corresponds to the problem solved.

1. number of Rs : number of Ts

2. number of Ts : vowels

3. consonants : vowels

4. consonants : total number of letters

Next, use the letters in the word **PROPORTION** to write a fraction for each ratio. Reduce the fraction to lowest terms. Find the fraction in the box on the right and write the corresponding letter on the correct space below.

5. consonants : total number of letters

6. vowels : consonants

7. number of Ps : total number of letters

8. number of Is : consonants

9. number of Ps : vowels

10. number of Ps and Os : total number of letters

Fraction Box

A = 1

B = $^1/_7$

C = $^2/_5$

D = $^3/_4$

E = $^3/_7$

N = $^1/_3$

O = $^2/_3$

P = $^1/_5$

S = $^1/_2$

T = $^3/_5$

U = $^1/_6$

W = $^1/_8$

Y = $^3/_8$

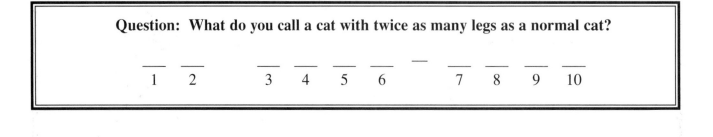

Question: What do you call a cat with twice as many legs as a normal cat?

$\overline{}$ $\overline{}$ $\overline{}$ $\overline{}$ $\overline{}$ $\overline{}$ $\overline{}$ $\overline{}$ $\overline{}$ $\overline{}$
 1   2   3   4   5   6   7   8   9   10

Focus: Setting up ratios in fractional form

The Very Best

Directions: Solve each proportion below and then replace the blank spaces below with the variable that matches each answer. The resulting message will be the answer to the riddle. Not all letters will be used to solve the riddle.

1. $\dfrac{5}{6} = \dfrac{e}{36}$

2. $\dfrac{4}{8} = \dfrac{i}{27}$

3. $\dfrac{3}{26} = \dfrac{9}{y}$

4. $\dfrac{n}{7} = \dfrac{15}{9}$

5. $\dfrac{4}{5} = \dfrac{s}{1.25}$

6. $\dfrac{3}{8} = \dfrac{27}{m}$

7. $\dfrac{L}{8.4} = \dfrac{3}{1.2}$

8. $\dfrac{9.3}{r} = \dfrac{.27}{.9}$

9. $\dfrac{1.7}{5.1} = \dfrac{.5}{v}$

10. $\dfrac{1.1}{3.3} = \dfrac{6.9}{w}$

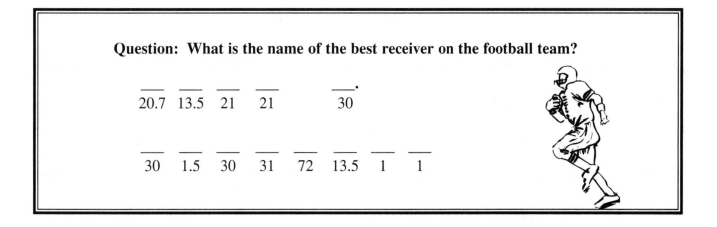

Question: What is the name of the best receiver on the football team?

$\overline{}\ \overline{}\ \overline{}\ \overline{}\ \ \ \ \overline{}\ .$
20.7 13.5 21 21   30

$\overline{}\ \overline{}\ \overline{}\ \overline{}\ \overline{}\ \overline{}\ \overline{}\ \overline{}$
30 1.5 30 31 72 13.5 1 1

Focus: Solving proportions

Fractions, Decimals, and Percents

Directions: Change each fraction into a decimal and a percent. Draw lines from the fractions to the correct decimal and then to the correct percents. Then, in the spaces below, write the letters from the decimal answer and the percent answer for each problem. The resulting message will be the answer to the riddle.

Fraction	Decimal	Percent
1. $5/8$	A. $.\overline{7}$	E. 40%
	B. $.8\overline{3}$	F. 25%
2. $9/18$	C. $.\overline{5}$	H. $66.\overline{6}$%
	E. $.5$	H. 62.5%
3. $5/6$	E. $.\overline{4}$	I. 55.5%
	F. $.65$	G. 65%
4. $6/9$	F. $.325$	G. 32.5%
	L. $.\overline{3}$	N. 17.8%
5. $7/21$	M. $.178$	O. $33.\overline{3}$%
	N. $.285$	O. $83.\overline{3}$%
6. $2/5$	N. $.16$	O. 125%
	O. $.25$	P. $77.\overline{7}$%
7. $5/4$	T. $.625$	R. $53.\overline{3}$%
	T. $.\overline{6}$	S. 1.78%
8. $8/15$	T. 1.25	S. 28.5%
	V. $.4$	T. 16%
9. $7/9$	W. $.5\overline{3}$	Y. 50%

Question: What do some musicians and Christmas fanatics have in common?

___ ___ ___ ___ ___ ___ ___ ___
1. decimal 1. percent 2. decimal 2. percent   3. decimal 3. percent 4. decimal 4. percent

___ ___ ___ ___ ___ ___
5. decimal 5. percent 6. decimal 6. percent 7. decimal 7. percent

(___) ___ ___ ___!
8. decimal 8. percent 9. decimal 9. percent

Focus: Changing fractions to decimals to percents

Don't Ruffle the Bird's Feathers

Directions: Complete the chart below. When you solve the two missing problems for each row, place the correct answers next to the letters. Then write the letters above the answers in the blanks below. The resulting words will be the completion of the rhyme. Not all letters will be used to solve the riddle.

Fraction	Decimal	Percent
1. I	.007	L
2. $^2/_3$	A	O
3. E	.75	B
4. D	F	6%
5. U	C	50%
6. A	$.\overline{5}$	P
7. $^1/_{25}$	H	I
8. R	.38	F
9. N	$.\overline{7}$	M
10. $^{15}/_{16}$	O	V
11. T	W	44%

Question: What does the star peacock of the basketball team expect during a game?

$\overline{}$ $\overline{}$ $\overline{}$ $\overline{}$ $\overline{}$ $\overline{}$
5/9   .7%   .9375   11/25   .9375   .06

$\overline{}$ $\overline{}$ $\overline{}$ $\overline{}$ — $\overline{}$ $\overline{}$
.04   66.7%   .9375   55.5%   .7%   .667

$\overline{}$ $\overline{}$ $\overline{}$ $\overline{}$ $\overline{}$ $\overline{}$ —
5/9   7/9   3/50   .06   .667   7/9

$\overline{}$ $\overline{}$ $\overline{}$ $\overline{}$!
38%   5/9   19/50   3/4

Focus: Changing fractions to decimals to percents

Chow Time

Directions: Solve each problem below. Write the variable on the lines above the correct answer in the question box. Be careful! Each answer must match exactly. Some answers will not have a space below. The resulting message will be the answer to the riddle.

1. 50% of 108 is M

2. 20% of 375 is W

3. N% of 8 is 6

4. A% of 48 is 18

5. F% of 15 is 12

6. 10% of L is 60

7. 10% of 45 is S

8. 5% of 1600 is O

9. 27 is 75% of D

10. 150% of R is 36

11. .4% of C is 1.44

12. 15% of 62 is T

13. 200% of E is 36

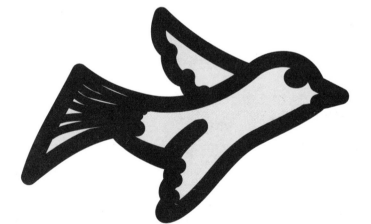

Question: What is a canary's favorite breakfast cereal?

___ ___ ___ ___ ___   ___ ___   ___ ___ ___ ___ ___
360 24   18 37.5% 54   80   80%   9.3   75   18   18   9.3

Focus: Solving percent problems

Pet-Pal Parlor

Directions: Mr. Paul Perfect owns the Pet-Pal Parlor. He needs to change the prices on some of his food in order to make money. Study the menu below and the changes on page 58. Find the percent of change in each of the prices. Round the answers to the nearest tenth of a percent. Find the answer to each problem in the answer box, and write the letter (which is next to it) on the blank space which contains the number of the problem. Not all letters will be used to solve the riddle.

Menu

Monkey Meals

Bow-wow Burger	$1.25
w/Cheese	$1.50
Meow-mostaccioli	$4.00
Sssss-spaghetti	$1.75
w/Meatballs	$2.00
Roar Ravioli	$3.30
Oink! Oink! Oysters	$9.00
Grrrr! Grilled Cheese	$3.60
Cheap Chicken	$4.80

Snake Side Orders

Caw! Cole Slaw	$ .25
Paws Potato Salad	$ .50

Panda Pops

Ribbit Root Beer	$ .80
Slithering Slurp	$ .80
Galloping Grape Soda	$ .80

Doggie Desserts

Chocolate Mooo! Mousse	$2.25
Tweet Tweet Twister	$1.00
Cock-a-Doodle Doo Doughnut	$ .50
Ruff! Rhubarb Pie	$ .80
Chocolate Cow Pie	$ .80
Flying Float	$1.00

Pet-Pal Parlor *(cont.)*

Price Changes

1.	Meow-mostaccioli	$5.00
2.	Grrrr! Grilled Cheese	$5.40
3.	Chocolate Mooo! Mousse	$2.00
4.	Tweet Tweet Twister	$ .75
5.	Cheap Chicken	$5.00
6.	Panda Pops	$1.10
7.	Flying Float	$ .60
8.	Roar Ravioli	$3.00
9.	Bow-wow Burger (no cheese)	$1.50
10.	Bow-wow Burger (with cheese)	$1.75
11.	Oink! Oink! Oysters	$11.00
12.	Chocolate Cow Pie	$1.25
13.	Caw! Cole Slaw	$ .19

Answer Box

Increases

4.2% = A

16.7% = D

20% = H

22.2% = I

25% = K

37.5% = N

50% = O

56.3% = R

Decreases

9.1% = S

11.1% = T

25% = U

24% = W

40% = Y

Question: How did the student answer when asked, "Why was the social studies teacher mad at you?"

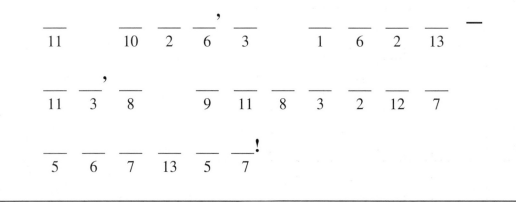

Focus: Finding percent increase and percent decrease

The Young Vampire

Directions: Arrange the following data (test scores) in the Frequency Table. Notice the frequency for each number, and find its corresponding letter in the Letter Bin. Write the letters in the letter column to find the first part of the answer to the riddle.

Question: Who did the vampire play with when he was younger?

Frequency Table			
Scores	**Tally**	**Frequency**	**Letter**
65			
68			
69			
78			
79			
85			
87			
88			
89			
90			
95			
97			
98			

Test Scores: 85, 85, 85, 85, 85, 79, 79, 79, 79, 87, 90, 90, 78, 78, 68, 69, 69, 85, 69, 68, 98, 90, 69, 68, 78, 68, 87, 97, 79, 69, 98, 90, 89, 89, 89, 97, 97, 68, 78, 78, 85, 69, 85, 65, 68, 68, 69, 87, 90, 85, 90, 88, 69, 88, 69, 78, 87, 97, 78, 90, 78, 90, 90, 79, 85, 97, 69, 90

Letter Bin

T = 1	**S** = 2
N = 3	**L** = 4
K = 5	**I** = 6
H = 7	**G** = 8
E = 10	**R** = 10
C = 0	

Using the same data, complete the chart below. Circle the letter that each number group reaches to find the last word of the riddle.

	1	2	3	4	5	6	7	8	9	10	11	12	13	14	15	16	17	18	19	20
60–69			X			J			G				P				D			
70–79		W		A					E				O	C		B				
80–89					Q				Z			F		Y				O		
90–99		M	N				H				L				K	R				

Focus: Organizing data in a frequency table and a chart

No Rest for the Weary

Directions: Find the mean of each set of numbers. Round the answer to the nearest tenth. Look for the letter in the letter bin to match your rounded answer. To solve the riddle, write the letters (in the spaces at the bottom of the page) which correspond to the problems that you just solved.

1. 10, 11, 12, 16, 18, 20   Mean =_____

2. 85, 42, 16, 32, 35   Mean =_____

3. 20, 14, 31, 9, 18, 42, 17   Mean =_____

4. 5, 6, 7, 8, 9, 10, 11, 12   Mean =_____

5. 15, 20, 25, 30, 35, 40   Mean =_____

6. 3, 13, 23, 33, 43   Mean =_____

7. 1, 4, 9, 16, 25, 36   Mean =_____

8. 2, 4, 6, 8, 10, 12, 14, 16   Mean =_____

9. 1, 3, 5, 7, 9, 11, 13, 15, 17, 19   Mean =_____

10. 2, 3, 5, 7, 11, 13, 17, 19, 23, 29   Mean =_____

Letter Bin	
E = 8.5	**R** = 15.2
E = 9	**S** = 21.6
E = 10	**T** = 23
L = 11	**T** = 27.5
M = 12.9	**U** = 31
N = 14.5	**V** = 42
O = 15	

Question: Where did the workaholic and his wife go on vacation?

__ __.
10   6

__ __ __ __ __ __ __ __
1   8   2   9   7   4   3   5

Focus: Calculating the mean from a set of data

Doggy Diagnosis

Directions: For each set of numbers find the mean, the mode, and the median, in that order. Be sure to look for the letters in the boxes below and round each answer to the nearest tenth if needed. To find the solution, read (horizontally) across the mean, mode, and median columns from 1–14.

Question: What did the veterinarian say when the woman brought in her dog who had swallowed a roll of film?

Numbers	Mean	Mode	Median
1. 78, 72, 65, 65, 70			
2. 53, 14, 14, 27, 67, 42, 14			
3. 85, 90, 90, 95			
4. 3, 15, 27, 90, 90			
5. 14, 90, 90, 90, 16, 14, 6, 8			
6. 49, 52, 65, 65, 76, 84			
7. 15, 15, 14, 14, 13, 17, 16			
8. 15, 18, 19, 16, 19, 15, 15, 20, 16			
9. 10, 8, 14, 14, 31, 41, 53, 65, 61			
10. 14.8, 19.2, 18.7, 15.8, 13			
11. 16.9, 16, 14.1, 9.2, 9.2, 17.8, 19			
12. 33.1, 34.9, 30, 32, 33, 34, 34			
13. 15, 17, 20, 24, 25, 10, 10, 10			
14. 17, 19, 18, 16, 15, 14, 20, 14, 20			

Mean Box		Mode Box		Median Box	
A = 16.3	I = 70	G = 34	P = 15	S = 17	L = 15
E = 16.4	K = 45	H = 9.2	R = 10	S = 33.1	N = 90
N = 50.75	L = 65.2	D = 65	T = 14	E = 65	O = 31
O = 17	N = 33	E = 14, 15	U = 14, 20	I = 16	T = 27
T = 14.6	V = 14.9	I = 90	N = none	O = 70	Y = 15.8
H = 90	W = 41				

Focus: Calculating the mean, median, and mode from given data sets

The Land Down Under

Directions: Arrange the test scores below in a stem and leaf plot from least to greatest. After organizing all of the data in the plot, count the number of leaves per stem. Then look below the chart to find the letter which corresponds to the number of leaves. Find the answer to the following question by writing the correct letter on the appropriate line.

Question: Where do Australian children go to play?

___

Test Scores: 96, 81, 79, 79, 100, 100, 93, 87, 62, 67, 91, 80, 91, 83, 47, 98, 93, 88, 88, 70, 75, 63, 63, 100, 57, 58, 96, 74

Stems	Leaves

Number of leaves	Letter

Letters

A=6	D=8	G=11	K=3	U=2
B=5	E=9	H=12	O=1	T=4
C=7	F=10	I=13		

Focus: Organizing data in a stem and leaf plot

Disguising Data Definitions

Directions: Read each definition below. Determine what word fits each description. (If you have difficulty thinking of the correct vocabulary word, look below the word find on page 64 for a list of words to use.) Finally, circle each word when you locate it in the word find.

1. the difference between the least and greatest numbers in a group of numbers:

   _____

2. the exact middle number in organized data:_____

3. the average of a set of numbers:_____

4. the number which appears most in a set of data:_____

5. a chart used to organize data that has the greatest place value as a stem and the smaller place

   value as leaves:_____

6. a chart used to organize data and to tally the frequency of the data:

   _____

7. a counting technique used in a frequency table:_____

8. a diagram which summarizes data by using the median, upper and lower quartiles, and outlier:

   _____

9. data which is more than 1.5 times the interquartile range away from the quartiles:

   _____

10. a group of numbers collected together to study:_____

11. the middle number in the upper half of the data:_____

12. ask a group of people questions for statistical information:_____

13. a random group used to test and predict what could happen:_____

14. a graph which shows the relationship between two groups of data:

   _____

Disguising Data Definitions *(cont.)*

Word Find

```
M T P P E R Q U A R T I L F S U
T O Y E G N A R E U V U E R T P
E L C T R A A M G S E Q U E L P
T P N I A I O I N R Y R U Q M E
S F E L E D N D A R Q Y P U A R
U E U E E E O E M F E P N E Z Q
R L O Q D M E A N V E E D N F U
V S U A T O L P R E T T A C S A
Y T T E A M P U S P A C T Y A R
D M L R T A S L E Y L L A T M T
N A I F A S B L E T O E L A P I
S R E K S I H W D N A X O B L L
L A R T T C S S C A T R P L E E
E T O L P F A E L D N A M E T S
```

Word List

box and whiskers	range
data	sample
frequency table	scatter plot
mean	stem and leaf plot
median	survey
mode	tally
outlier	upper quartile

Focus: Identifying statistical terms

64

Heard It Through the Grapevine

Directions: Solve each permutation, combination, or factorial. Find each answer in the Letter Box, and notice the letter next to it. Write that letter on the blank space that contains the number of the problem. Some letters have been done for you. The resulting message will be the answer to the riddle.

1. P(6, 3)

2. P(8, 4)

3. 7!

4. P(6, 6)

5. P(7, 5)

6. C(6, 3)

7. 6!

8. C(8, 4)

9. C(5, 5)

10. C(7, 5)

11. 9!

12. P(9, 5)

13. C(9, 5)

14. P(3, 2)

Letter Box	
N = 126	F = 2520
A = 720	P = 20
S = 6	O = 5040
U = 15,120	G = 70
E = 1680	H = 120
R = 1	B = 362,880
K = 21	

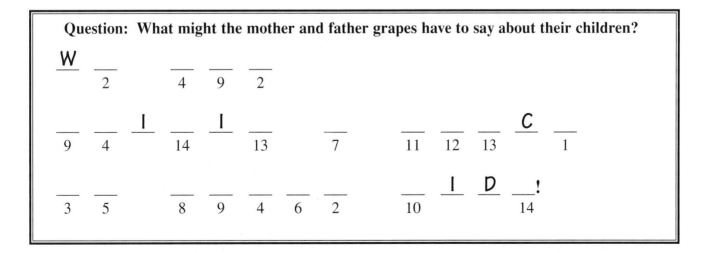

Question: What might the mother and father grapes have to say about their children?

W __ __ __ __
  2   4 9 2

__ __ I __ I __   __ __ __ C __
9 4   14 13   7   11 12 13   1

__ __ __ __ __ __ __   __ I D __!
3 5   8 9 4 6 2   10   14

Focus: Solving permutations, combinations, and factorials

Probably Probability

Directions: Follow each set of instructions below. Convert the fractional answer into a decimal, rounding to the nearest hundredth. Add up all of the decimal answers.

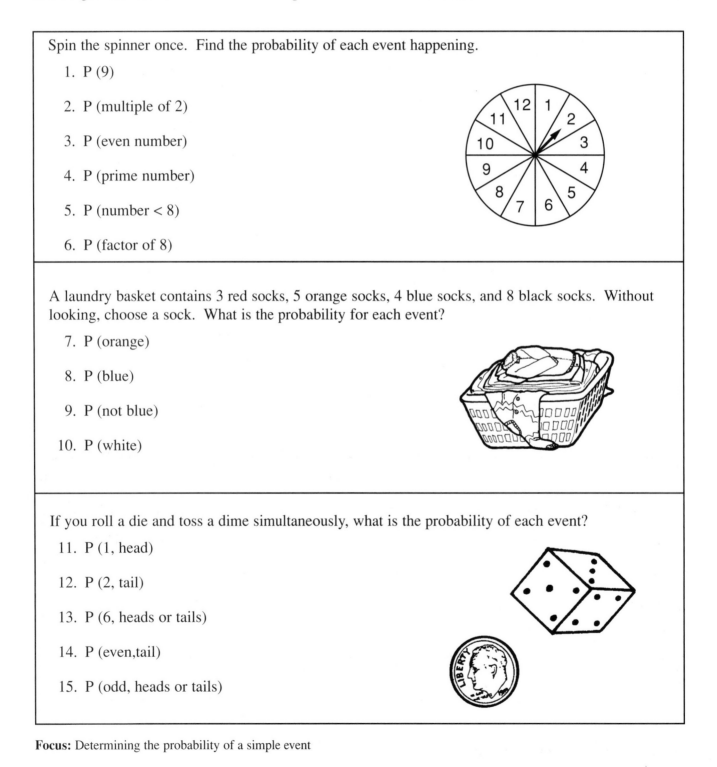

Spin the spinner once. Find the probability of each event happening.

1. P (9)

2. P (multiple of 2)

3. P (even number)

4. P (prime number)

5. P (number < 8)

6. P (factor of 8)

A laundry basket contains 3 red socks, 5 orange socks, 4 blue socks, and 8 black socks. Without looking, choose a sock. What is the probability for each event?

7. P (orange)

8. P (blue)

9. P (not blue)

10. P (white)

If you roll a die and toss a dime simultaneously, what is the probability of each event?

11. P (1, head)

12. P (2, tail)

13. P (6, heads or tails)

14. P (even, tail)

15. P (odd, heads or tails)

Focus: Determining the probability of a simple event

Know the Terms

Directions: Below you will find some mathematical terms used in probability and statistics. Search the puzzle for each of the words. When you find one of the vocabulary words, circle it.

```
G  R  A  H  P  I  L  T  U  O  R  T  X  E  O  Y  N
C  T  N  E  D  N  E  P  E  D  N  I  R  P  P  C  O
E  M  E  L  M  A  R  G  A  I  D  E  E  R  T  N  I
C  D  M  I  A  N  O  D  F  R  I  R  O  I  N  E  T
A  I  A  T  E  V  E  N  T  L  M  B  R  H  E  U  A
P  P  R  R  M  U  Q  E  T  U  A  N  A  P  D  Q  T
S  E  G  A  O  E  R  U  T  B  N  A  T  A  N  E  U
E  Z  O  U  C  U  O  A  I  G  A  E  O  R  E  R  A
L  I  T  Q  T  N  T  L  N  O  I  M  I  G  P  F  V
P  N  S  C  U  I  I  L  T  G  D  E  T  D  E  S  E
M  A  I  Y  O  T  I  S  I  R  E  R  A  M  D  M  R
A  G  H  N  Y  H  R  M  A  E  M  T  R  D  O  R  A
S  R  E  K  S  I  H  W  D  N  A  X  O  B  B  D  G
D  O  D  S  T  E  M  A  N  D  L  E  A  F  P  E  E
```

Terms

average	extreme	median	permutation	stem and leaf
box and	frequency	mode	probability	tree diagram
whiskers	graph	odds	quartile	
data	histogram	organize	range	
dependent	independent	outcome	ratio	
event	mean	outlier	sample space	

Focus: Becoming familiar with statistical and probability terminology

What's Left?

Directions: Find and cross out all of the listed geometrical terms. (Every word is in the puzzle. For example, rectangle and angle are two separate words.) When all of the terms have been found, the remaining letters in the puzzle will form an answer to the riddle. The stars in the puzzle represent spaces in the answer.

```
L A S R E V S N A R T V A F T
A E R O I R E T N I A E R A R
R E L G N A I R T ★ T R N P A
E R A U Q S D D T U I T N O G
T N E U R G N O C I ★ E U L C
A P ★ E L G N A A L C X R Y T
L N L X R V O L U M E A ★ G N
I O T T H G E ★ E F D E L O E
U G A E C T E O S I R S G N M
Q A R R S ★ I D U ★ F A N I G
E T O I G N U S T R T B I R E
R N T O E C O N B C ★ I D A S
H E C R R A Y G O T ★ M N L S
O P A D E U R L A G S T O I U
M A R I C ' A V I X A E P M P
B R T O T T T L I N E C S I P
U A O Z A N N A E ★ D H E S L
S L R E N I E N R B I E R D E
E L P P G O M O U S M P R I M
E E N A L P E G S R A T O A E
B L R R E D L A A I R A C M N
I N E T ★ I P I E G Y G S E T
S U L M - M M D M H P O T T A
E H U I O P O I N T N N G E R
C I R C L E C G E O M E T R Y
T N E C A J D A ★ H T G N E L
```

Acute	Midpoint
Adjacent	Obtuse
Angle	Octagon
Area	Parallel
Base	Pentagon
Bisect	Plane
Circle	Point
Compass	Polygon
Complementary	Protractor
Cone	Pyramid
Congruent	Radius
Corresponding	Ray
Cylinder	Rectangle
Decagon	Rhombus
Degree	Right
Diagonal	Ruler
Diameter	Segment
Equilateral	Similar
Exterior	Square
Geometry	Supplementary
Heptagon	Transversal
Hexagon	Trapezoid
Interior	Triangle
Length	Vertex
Line	Vertical
Measure	Volume

Question: Why was the math teacher mad at you?

Answer: _____

Focus: Identifying geometrical terms

Food for Thought

Directions: Each pair of angles is either vertical, complementary, or supplementary. Find the degree measure of each angle. On the way, you will find the variable in each problem. To find the answer to the question, write the variable on its matching line at the bottom of the page.

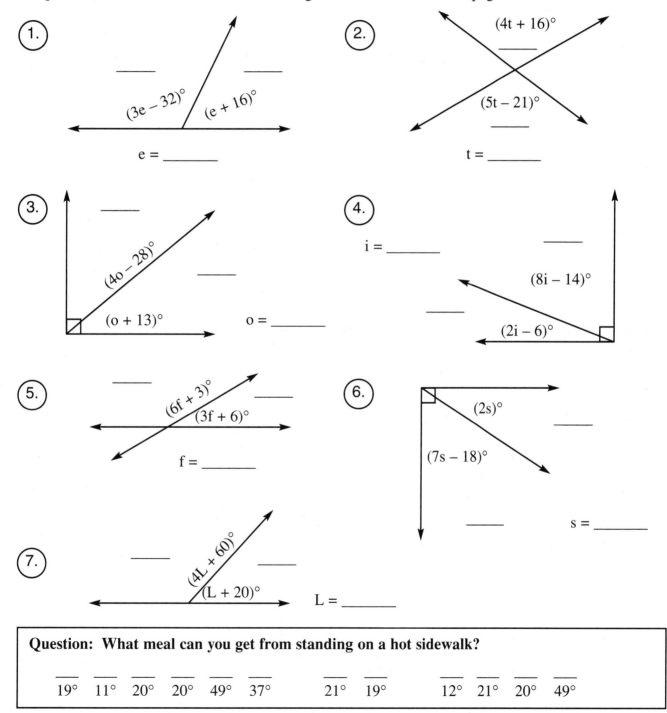

Question: What meal can you get from standing on a hot sidewalk?

$\underline{\quad}$ $\underline{\quad}$ $\underline{\quad}$ $\underline{\quad}$ $\underline{\quad}$ $\underline{\quad}$ $\underline{\quad}$ $\underline{\quad}$ $\underline{\quad}$ $\underline{\quad}$ $\underline{\quad}$ $\underline{\quad}$
19° 11° 20° 20° 49° 37°   21° 19°   12° 21° 20° 49°

Focus: Identifying angle relationships

The Square Team

Directions: There are three correct answers for each problem. Circle the single INCORRECT statement. The letters next to the incorrect answers will provide the solution to the riddle when they are placed on the blank lines, which match the problem numbers, below.

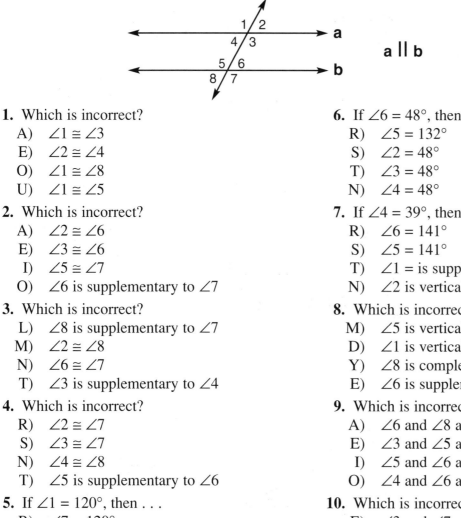

a ∥ b

1. Which is incorrect?
- A) ∠1 ≅ ∠3
- E) ∠2 ≅ ∠4
- O) ∠1 ≅ ∠8
- U) ∠1 ≅ ∠5

2. Which is incorrect?
- A) ∠2 ≅ ∠6
- E) ∠3 ≅ ∠6
- I) ∠5 ≅ ∠7
- O) ∠6 is supplementary to ∠7

3. Which is incorrect?
- L) ∠8 is supplementary to ∠7
- M) ∠2 ≅ ∠8
- N) ∠6 ≅ ∠7
- T) ∠3 is supplementary to ∠4

4. Which is incorrect?
- R) ∠2 ≅ ∠7
- S) ∠3 ≅ ∠7
- N) ∠4 ≅ ∠8
- T) ∠5 is supplementary to ∠6

5. If ∠1 = 120°, then . . .
- R) ∠7 = 120°
- S) ∠6 = 120°
- T) ∠2 = 60°
- N) ∠4 = 60

6. If ∠6 = 48°, then . . .
- R) ∠5 = 132°
- S) ∠2 = 48°
- T) ∠3 = 48°
- N) ∠4 = 48°

7. If ∠4 = 39°, then . . .
- R) ∠6 = 141°
- S) ∠5 = 141°
- T) ∠1 = is supplementary to ∠4
- N) ∠2 is vertical to ∠4

8. Which is incorrect?
- M) ∠5 is vertical to ∠7
- D) ∠1 is vertical to ∠3
- Y) ∠8 is complementary to ∠5
- E) ∠6 is supplementary to ∠7

9. Which is incorrect?
- A) ∠6 and ∠8 are vertical angles
- E) ∠3 and ∠5 are alternate interior angles
- I) ∠5 and ∠6 are vertical angles
- O) ∠4 and ∠6 are alternate interior angles

10. Which is incorrect?
- E) ∠3 and ∠7 are corresponding angles
- F) ∠3 and ∠6 are alternate interior angles
- G) ∠5 and ∠1 are corresponding angles
- H) ∠5 + ∠2 = 180°

Question: What professional football team is the square of a prime number?

—— —— —— —— ——   —— —— —— —— —— ——
10   1   4   6   8   3   9   3   2   7   5

Focus: Identifying angle relationships when parallel lines are cut by a transversal

Mystery Name

Directions: Find the missing angle measure in each triangle. When you have completed a problem, look at the blank lines at the bottom of the page. Notice if any of the angle degrees of the letters match the degrees under the blank lines. If they do, write the letter of the angle on the line. The resulting message will be the answer to the riddle.

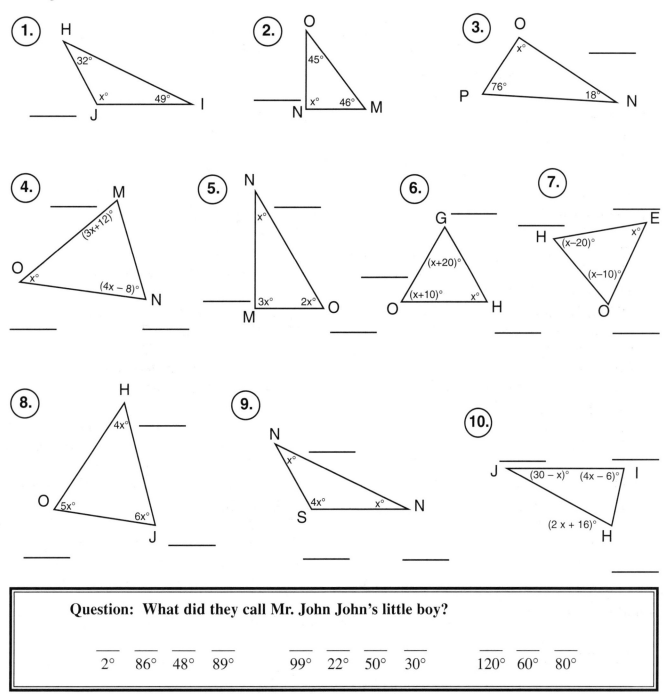

Question: What did they call Mr. John John's little boy?

___ ___ ___ ___   ___ ___ ___ ___   ___ ___ ___
2°   86° 48° 89°   99° 22° 50° 30°   120° 60° 80°

Focus: Finding the degrees of missing angle measurements in triangles

Vacation Destination

Directions: In each problem there are congruent triangles with three answers. Decide which answer has corresponding parts that are congruent. Notice the letter next to each correct answer. Write that letter on the blank line which corresponds to the problem you have just solved. (There will only be one correct answer per problem.)

1. △ABC = △DEF   (D) ∠D ≅ ∠C   (E) $\overline{BC}$ ≅ $\overline{EF}$ (F) $\overline{CA}$ ≅ $\overline{DE}$

2. △RST = △UWV   (A) ∠T ≅ ∠U   (E) $\overline{RS}$ ≅ $\overline{WU}$ (I) $\overline{TS}$ ≅ $\overline{UW}$

3. △MQB = △XPR   (H) ∠B ≅ ∠R   (G) $\overline{XR}$ ≅ $\overline{QM}$ (I) ∠Q ≅ ∠R

4. △TOM = △JAY   (S) ∠JYA ≅ ∠OTM   (U) ∠OMT ≅ ∠AJY   (T) $\overline{JA}$ ≅ $\overline{OT}$

5. (R) △BAD ≅ △JOY   (S) △BAD ≅ △YOJ   (T) △ABD ≅ △OJY

6. (A) ∠JUM ≅ ∠HIP   (E) $\overline{UM}$ ≅ $\overline{PI}$ (I) $\overline{JU}$ ≅ $\overline{HI}$

7. (C) $\overline{BR}$ ≅ $\overline{YR}$ (D) ∠BIR ≅ ∠DRY   (G) ∠BRI ≅ ∠RDY

8. (P) ∠DNS ≅ ∠ANS   (R) △ASN ≅ △DNS   (T) △ANS ≅ △DNS

9. △KTU = △RCS   (U) △TUK ≅ △CRS   (E) △UKC ≅ △SRT   (O) △KTU ≅ △RCS

10. △DOG ≅ △CAT   (K) ∠OGD ≅ ∠ATC   (I) ∠OGD ≅ ∠TAC   (T) ∠ODG ≅ ∠CTA

Question: Where is Sylvester Stallone's favorite vacation spot?

$\underline{\hspace{1.2em}}$ $\underline{\hspace{1.2em}}$ $\underline{\hspace{1.2em}}$ $\underline{\hspace{1.2em}}$ $\underline{\hspace{1.2em}}$ $\underline{\hspace{1.2em}}$ $\underline{\hspace{1.2em}}$ $\underline{\hspace{1.2em}}$ $\underline{\hspace{1.2em}}$ $\underline{\hspace{1.2em}}$
    4   3   1   8   9   7   10   6   2   5

Focus: Identifying corresponding parts of congruent triangles

All Aboard!

Directions: Complete each conditional statement. You are given the hypothesis, and you must find the correct conclusion to make the statement true. When you find the correct conclusion, circle the letters in front of it. When you have completed all seven, the letters will form a phrase that answers the question at the bottom of the page.

1. If 2 ∠'s add up to 90, then

    TH both ∠'s = 90
    TO the ∠'s are supplementary
    TR the ∠'s are complementary

2. If it is cloudy outside, then

    UE it will rain
    AI it might rain
    US it won't rain

3. If you see a person with long hair, then

    NY it could be a male
    LS it must be a female
    LO it must be a male

4. If a figure is a triangle, then

    ES each ∠ = 180
    OU all ∠'s add up to 180
    AR all ∠'s add up to 90

5. If 2 lines are parallel and are cut by a transversal, then

    RB the corresponding ∠'s are equal
    TR all ∠'s must be equal
    RD all ∠'s on the same side of the transversal are always equal

6. If it is raining while the sun is out, then

    OD you are on another planet
    LO there must be a rainbow
    RA there will sometimes be a rainbow in the sky

7. If a number is divisible by 2 and 3, then

    IN it must be divisible by 6
    ON it might be divisible by 5
    ID it must not be divisible by 6

Question: What is the slogan for the railroad engineering school?

_____

Focus: Writing true conditional statements

Shop 'Til You Drop

Directions: Find the area and perimeter of each polygon. When you have found both answers, look in the box to the right, and find the letter which is next to your answer. To answer the riddle, fill in the blanks at the bottom of the page. Under each blank there is a number for the problem number, and a letter A (for area) or P (for perimeter). Write the correct letter in each space. (For example, 1A would be the area answer letter for problem number one.) Some answers will not have a space in the puzzle.

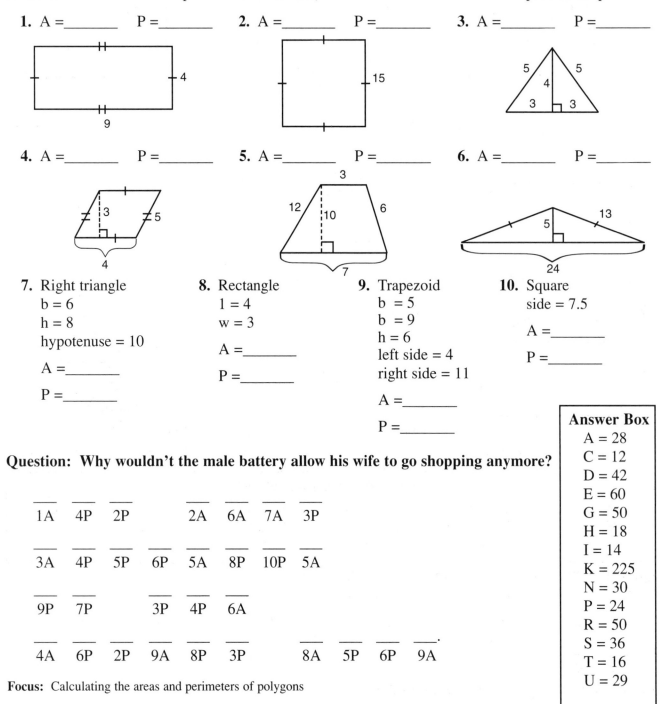

1. A = _____ P = _____

2. A = _____ P = _____

3. A = _____ P = _____

4. A = _____ P = _____

5. A = _____ P = _____

6. A = _____ P = _____

7. Right triangle
b = 6
h = 8
hypotenuse = 10

A = _____

P = _____

8. Rectangle
l = 4
w = 3

A = _____

P = _____

9. Trapezoid
b = 5
b = 9
h = 6
left side = 4
right side = 11

A = _____

P = _____

10. Square
side = 7.5

A = _____

P = _____

Answer Box
A = 28
C = 12
D = 42
E = 60
G = 50
H = 18
I = 14
K = 225
N = 30
P = 24
R = 50
S = 36
T = 16
U = 29

Question: Why wouldn't the male battery allow his wife to go shopping anymore?

___ ___ ___   ___ ___ ___ ___
1A   4P   2P   2A   6A   7A   3P

___ ___ ___ ___ ___ ___ ___ ___
3A   4P   5P   6P   5A   8P   10P 5A

___ ___   ___ ___ ___
9P   7P   3P   4P   6A

___ ___ ___ ___ ___ ___   ___ ___ ___ ___.
4A   6P   2P   9A   8P   3P   8A   5P   6P   9A

Focus: Calculating the areas and perimeters of polygons

Speedy the Squirrel

Directions: Find the area of each figure below. Then find each answer in the Answer Box, and notice the letter next to it. Write that letter in the blank at the bottom of the page that contains the number of the problem. The resulting message will be the answer to the riddle.

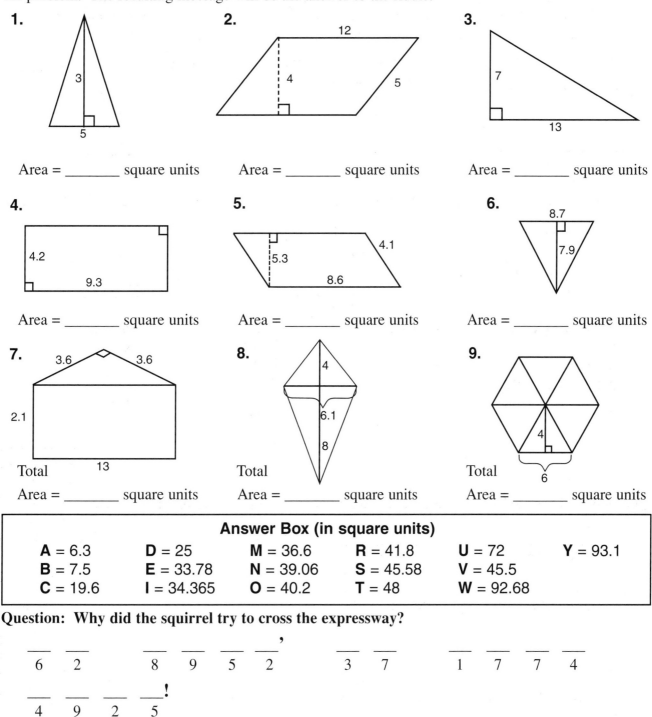

1.

Area = _____ square units

2.

12

4

5

Area = _____ square units

3.

7

13

Area = _____ square units

3

5

4.

4.2

9.3

Area = _____ square units

5.

5.3

8.6

4.1

Area = _____ square units

6.

8.7

7.9

Area = _____ square units

7.

3.6   3.6

2.1

13

Total
Area = _____ square units

8.

4

6.1

8

Total
Area = _____ square units

9.

4

6

Total
Area = _____ square units

Answer Box (in square units)					
A = 6.3	**D** = 25	**M** = 36.6	**R** = 41.8	**U** = 72	**Y** = 93.1
B = 7.5	**E** = 33.78	**N** = 39.06	**S** = 45.58	**V** = 45.5	
C = 19.6	**I** = 34.365	**O** = 40.2	**T** = 48	**W** = 92.68	

Question: Why did the squirrel try to cross the expressway?

___ ___   ___ ___ ___ ___ ,   ___ ___   ___ ___ ___ ___
 6   2   8   9   5   2   3   7   1   7   7   4

___ ___ ___ ___ !
 4   9   2   5

Focus: Calculating the areas of triangles and parallelograms

Check, please!

Directions: Find the area and perimeter of each trapezoid. Look for the answer in the Answer Box below and then notice the letter next to it. To solve the riddle, write that letter in the blank space at the bottom of the page that contains the number/letter of the problem. (For example 1A in the riddle represents the area for problem 1. Find the area and its letter in the answer box.) Some answers will not have a space in the puzzle.

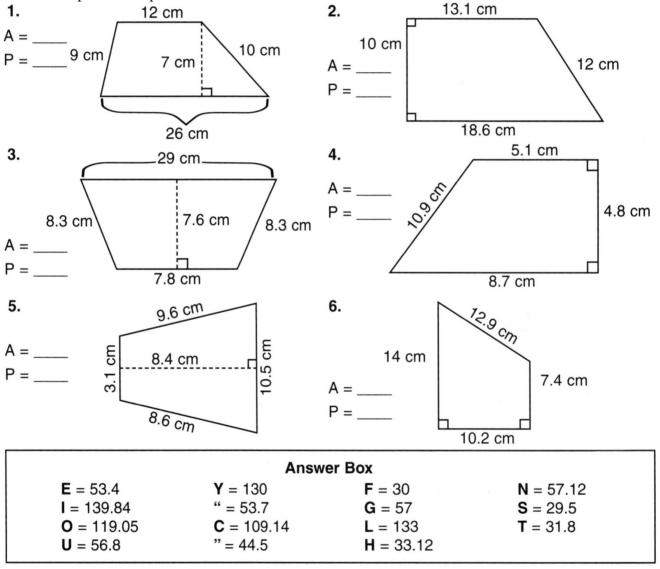

1.
A = _____
P = _____
12 cm
9 cm
7 cm
10 cm
26 cm

2.
A = _____
P = _____
13.1 cm
10 cm
12 cm
18.6 cm

3.
A = _____
P = _____
29 cm
8.3 cm
7.6 cm
8.3 cm
7.8 cm

4.
A = _____
P = _____
5.1 cm
10.9 cm
4.8 cm
8.7 cm

5.
A = _____
P = _____
9.6 cm
3.1 cm
8.4 cm
10.5 cm
8.6 cm

6.
A = _____
P = _____
12.9 cm
14 cm
7.4 cm
10.2 cm

Answer Box			
E = 53.4	**Y** = 130	**F** = 30	**N** = 57.12
I = 139.84	" = 53.7	**G** = 57	**S** = 29.5
O = 119.05	**C** = 109.14	**L** = 133	**T** = 31.8
U = 56.8	" = 44.5	**H** = 33.12	

Question: What did the patron say to the chef upon tasting the omelet?

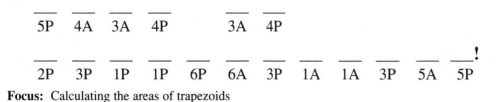

___ ___ ___ ___   ___ ___
5P   4A   3A   4P   3A   4P

___ ___ ___ ___ ___ ___ ___ ___ ___ ___ ___ ___!
2P   3P   1P   1P   6P   6A   3P   1A   1A   3P   5A   5P

Focus: Calculating the areas of trapezoids

A Painful Problem

Directions: Solve each area or circumference problem below. Circle the correct answer and then write the letter from the answer on the corresponding space below. The resulting message will be the answer to the riddle. Use 3.14 for π.

1. Find the area of this circle.

2 in

(L) 3.14 in²   (M) 12.56 in²
(N) 25.12 in²   (O) 50.24 in²

2. Find the circumference of this circle.

4 in

(L) 3.14 in   (M) 12.56 in
(N) 25.12 in   (O) 50.24 in

3. Find the circumference of this circle.

6.4 cm

(A) 10.048 cm   (E) 20.096 cm
(I) 40.192 cm   (O) 32.1536 cm

4. Find the area of a circle with a radius of 2.5 m.

(A) 3.925 m²   (E) 7.85 m²
(I) 15.7 m²   (O) 19.625 m²

5. Find the circumference of a circle with a radius of 2.5 m.

(A) 3.925 m   (E) 7.85 m
(W) 15.7 m   (Y) 19.625 m

Question: What did the cat say when the candy that she ate hurt her tooth?

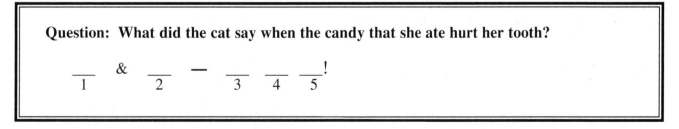

$\underline{}$ & $\underline{}$ — $\underline{}$ $\underline{}$ $\underline{}$!
  1   2   3   4   5

Focus: Calculating the areas and circumferences of circles

Corny Acorns

Directions: For problems 1–4, use the rectangular prism to answer each question. For problems 5–7, use the triangular prism to answer each question. Choose the correct answer, and write the letter in the space which is labeled with the matching problem number. The resulting message will be the answer to the riddle.

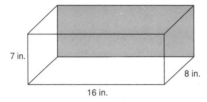

1. The area of the front face is . . .

    (A) 212 in²   (Y) 128 in²   (U) 256 in²   (E) 112 in²   (O) 128 in²   (I) 256 in²

2. The area of the left-hand face is . . .

    (H) 49 in²   (J) 156 in²   (K) 112 in²   (L) 49 in²   (M) 56 in²   (N) 112 in²

3. The area of the top face is . . .

    (S) 56 in²   (A) 112 in²   (T) 428 in²   (R) 56 in²   (N) 112 in²   (E) 128 in²

4. The total surface area of this rectangular prism is . . .

    (N) 31 in²   (S) 296 in²   (R) 592 in²   (T) 896 in²

5. The area of the bottom of this triangular prism is . . .

    (S) 120 ft²   (N) 187.5 ft²   (T) 375 ft²   (L) 120 ft²   (R) 187.5 ft²   (M) 675 ft²

6. The area of the triangular side of this roof is . . .

    (Y) 30 ft²   (A) 160 ft²   (E) 920 ft²   (I) 130 ft²   (O) 60 ft²   (U) 120 ft²

7. The area of the back face of this triangular prism is . . .

    (T) 200 ft²   (S) 875 ft²   (L) 1375 ft²   (M) 1200 ft²   (Y) 275 ft²   (R) 375 ft²

8. Find the total area of this triangular prism.

    (H) 925 ft²   (I) 1925 ft²   (G) 1045 ft²   (K) 1165 ft²

Question: What math word do acorns say when they grow up?

    <u>   </u>   <u>   </u>   <u>   </u>   <u>   </u>   <u>   </u>   <u>   </u>   <u>   </u>   <u>   </u>

     8   1   6   2   3   5   4   7

Focus: Calculating the surface areas of prisms

Use this guide when needed to help you with the brain teaser activities on pages 4–78.

Table of Contents

❏ Order of Operations

The order of operations rule is a rule designed to assure that every mathematical problem has its own answer. Sometimes a problem has more than one operation, and in order to guarantee a unique solution to the expression we must follow the order of operations pattern. For example, without order of operations, look what might happen:

With Rule:
9 + 6 x 2 (Multiply first.)
9 + 12 (Then add.)
 21

Without Rule:
9 + 6 x 2 (Add first.)
15 x 2 (Then multiply.)
 30

Order of Operations:

1. Do all operations inside the **PA**rentheses or brackets first. Start with the innermost parentheses.

2. Multiply out any of the **PO**wers. ($2^3 = 8$)

3. Solve any **M**ultiplication and **D**ivision expressions from left to right.

4. Solve the remaining **A**ddition and **S**ubtraction expressions from left to right.

You might want to try this memory device, or create one of your own, for learning the order of operations.

PAula **PO**ured **M**ilk **D**own **A**lexander's **S**horts!

❏ Translating Phrases into Algebraic Expressions

In algebra, we like to simplify words into mathematical symbols when possible. The following common algebraic expressions which are used throughout this book:

x – 4

some number minus four
some number decreased by four
four less than a number

4 – x

four minus some number
four decreased by a number
subtract a number from four

x ÷ 9

the quotient of a number and nine
a number divided by nine

9 ÷ x

the quotient of nine and a number
nine divided by a number

n + 10

the sum of a number and ten
a number plus ten
ten more than a number

5n or n x 5

five times a number
the product of a number and five

❏ Evaluating Expressions

A mathematical expression can be evaluated when a numerical value is substituted in place of the variable(s) in the expression.

Example:

Find the value of $2 + (a - b)$ if $a = 6$ and $b = 5$.

First replace the a in the expression with the value 6, and replace the b in the equation with the value 5. Now the expression should read: $2 + (6 - 5)$

Now solve every expression following the order of operations rule.
Begin by subtracting $6 - 5$, which equals 1. Then finish the problem, $2 + 1 = 3$.

❏ Properties of Addition and Multiplication

Commutative Property of Addition
For all real numbers a, b, then
$a + b = b + a$
example: $3 + 5 = 5 + 3$
$8 = 8$

Commutative Property of Multiplication
For all real numbers a, b, then
$a \times b = b \times a$
example: $3 \times 5 = 5 \times 3$
$15 = 15$

Associative Property of Addition
For all real numbers c, d, e, then
$c + (d + e) = (c + d) + e$
example: $4 + (8 + 2) = (4 + 8) + 2$
$4 + 10 = 12 + 2$
$14 = 14$

Associative Property of Multiplication
For all real numbers c, d, e, then
$c (d \times e) = (c \times d) \times e$
example: $4 \times (8 \times 2) = (4 \times 8) \times 2$
$4 \times 16 = 32 \times 2$
$64 = 64$

Identity Property of Addition
For any real number n, then
$n + 0 = n$
example: $9 + 0 = 9$

Identity Property of Multiplication
For any real number n, then
$n \times 1 = n$
example: $9 \times 1 = 9$

Distributive Property
For all real numbers, f, g, h, then
$f \times (g + h) = f \times g + f \times h$
example: $6 \times (1 + 7) = 6 \times 1 + 6 \times 7$
$6 \times 8 = 6 + 42$
$48 = 48$

Multiplicative Property of Zero
For any real number m, then
$m \times 0 = 0$
example: $99 \times 0 = 0$
or
$0 \times 99 = 0$

❑ Comparing and Ordering Integers

-10 -9 -8 -7 -6 -5 -4 -3 -2 -1 0 1 2 3 4 5 6 7 8 9 10

One method for understanding how to compare integers is simply to refer to a number line. A number line extends indefinitely in both directions. As we move to the right the numbers become larger, and as we move to the left the numbers become smaller.

Example: -7 is to the left of -5; therefore, -7 is less than -5 so -7 < -5

Or, -5 is to the right of -7; therefore, -5 is greater than -7 so -5 > -7

Example: Arrange 13, 5, -9, 0, 12, -20, and 2 in order from smallest to largest.
-20, -9, 0, 2, 5, 12, 13

❑ Adding and Subtracting Integers

To add integers with the same sign, add the two numbers together, keeping a positive sign if both are positive, keeping a negative sign if both are negative.

Examples: 2 + 3 = 5
-2 + -3 = -5

To add integers with different signs, subtract the two numbers, and keep the sign of the number with the greater absolute value.

Examples: -2 + 3 = 1
2 + -3 = -1

To subtract integers, change the problem to an equivalent addition problem by substituting the second number's additive inverse. If x – y, then change it to x + (-y). However, if you are subtracting a negative, the double negative actually means "take the opposite of the negative" which would be positive. So, if x – (-y), then change it to x + y.

Examples: 7 – 12   -5 – (-8)   -8 – 8
                    7 + (-12) = –5   -5 + 8 = 3   -8 + (-8) = -16

❑ Multiplying and Dividing Integers

The rules for multiplying and dividing integers are best learned when they are committed to memory.

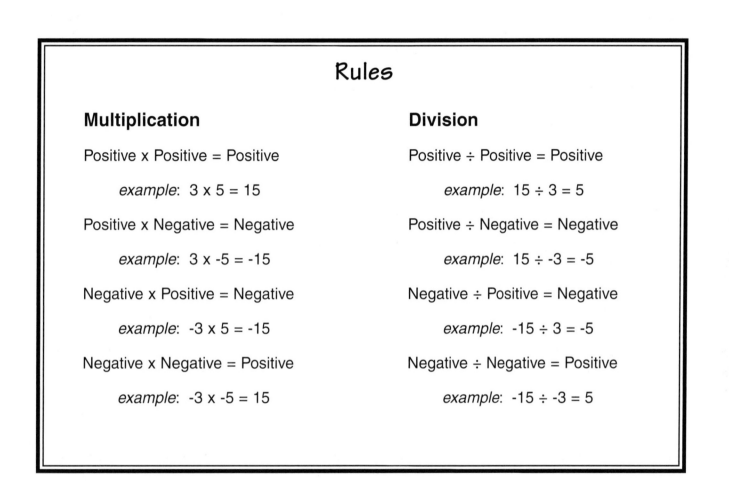

Rules	
Multiplication	**Division**
Positive x Positive = Positive	Positive ÷ Positive = Positive
example: 3 x 5 = 15	*example*: 15 ÷ 3 = 5
Positive x Negative = Negative	Positive ÷ Negative = Negative
example: 3 x -5 = -15	*example*: 15 ÷ -3 = -5
Negative x Positive = Negative	Negative ÷ Positive = Negative
example: -3 x 5 = -15	*example*: -15 ÷ 3 = -5
Negative x Negative = Positive	Negative ÷ Negative = Positive
example: -3 x -5 = 15	*example*: -15 ÷ -3 = 5

❑ Equations

An equation is a mathematical sentence which contains an expression and an equal sign. The equations below are solved by using inverse operations.

Example: Addition Equation

$$m + 6 = 12$$

Inverse Step—Subtraction

Solution: $m + 6 = 12$

$$\underline{\quad -6 \quad -6 \quad} \quad \leftarrow\text{Step: Subtract 6}$$

$$m = 6 \quad \leftarrow\text{Answer}$$

Example: Subtraction Equation

$$h - 4 = 18$$

Inverse Step—Addition

Solution: $h - 4 = 18$

$$\underline{\quad +4 \quad +4 \quad} \quad \leftarrow\text{Step: Add 4}$$

$$h = 22 \quad \leftarrow\text{Answer}$$

Example: Multiplication Equation

$$6y = 24$$

Inverse Step—Division

Solution: $6y = 24$

$$\frac{6y}{6} = \frac{24}{6} \quad \leftarrow\text{Step: Divide by 6}$$

$$y = 4 \quad \leftarrow\text{Answer}$$

Example: Division Equation

$$m \div 3 = 14$$

Inverse Step—Multiplication

Solution: $\dfrac{m}{3} = 14$

$$3\left(\frac{m}{3}\right) = (14)\,(3) \quad \leftarrow\text{Step: Multiply by 3}$$

$$m = 42 \quad \leftarrow\text{Answer}$$

❑ Addition and Subtraction Inequalities

Inequalities are similar to equations in the way they are solved. However, there may be more than one answer to make an inequality sentence correct.

Example: f + 5 < 12

$$\begin{array}{r} -5 \quad -5 \\ \hline f \quad < 7 \end{array}$$

So, the answer is f < 7 or {. . . -1, 0, 1, 2, 3, 4, 5, 6}.

Example: t - 16 ≥ 21

$$\begin{array}{r} +16 \quad +16 \\ \hline t \quad \geq 37 \end{array}$$

So, the answer is t ≥ 37 or {37, 38, 39, 40, . . . }.

❑ Multiplication and Division Inequalities

When solving multiplication and division inequalities involving negatives, there are some special rules to remember. The most important rule is, if you multiply or divide by a negative number (if there is a negative number in the step), the inequality sign must reverse its direction.

Example: m ÷ 11 ≤ -2

$$\begin{array}{ll} \text{x 11} \quad \text{x 11} & \text{Positive in step} \\ \hline \text{m} \leq -22 & \text{Sign does not reverse} \end{array}$$

Example: g x 3 > -24

$$\begin{array}{ll} \div 3 \quad \div 3 & \text{Positive in step} \\ \hline \text{g} \quad > \quad -8 & \text{Sign does not reverse} \end{array}$$

Example: m ÷ (-11) ≤ 2

$$\begin{array}{ll} \text{x -11} \quad \text{x-11} & \text{Negative in step} \\ \hline \text{m} \quad \geq -22 & \text{Sign must reverse} \end{array}$$

Example: g x (-3) > -24

$$\begin{array}{ll} \div -3 \quad \div -3 & \text{Negative in step} \\ \hline \text{g} \quad < \quad 8 & \text{Sign must reverse} \end{array}$$

❏ Divisibility Rules

The divisibility rules are simply tools to make dividing easier. If one can memorize the rules of divisibility, factoring can be done in a faster, more efficient manner.

A number is divisible by

2,   if the number is even.

3,   if the sum of the digits add up to a number divisible by three.

5,   if the digit in the ones place is a 0 or a 5.

6,   if the number is divisible by 2 and 3.

10,   if the digit in the ones place is a 0.

❏ Factor Trees

A factor tree is a method of breaking apart a number or an expression into its prime factorization. In other words, a factor tree can break an expression apart showing all of the prime numbers which are multiplied together to form the expression.

Example: Find the prime factorization of the number 150.

Solution:

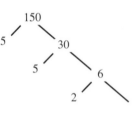

Answer:

2 x 3 x 5 x 5

❏ G.C.F. (Greatest Common Factor)

The greatest common factor (G. C. F) between numbers is exactly as the title reads. One is looking for the largest factor which is common among each of the numbers or monomials.

Example: Find the G.C.F. between 36d, 18de, 45d²e.

Solution: Use a factor to find the prime factorization for each. Then find each of the terms which all three monomials have in common. Finally, multiply these terms together for your G.C.F.

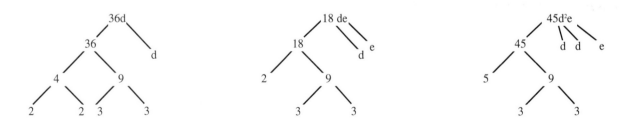

Answer: Each has two 3's in common and a d. So the G.C.F. = 3 x 3 x d = 9d.

❑ Least Common Multiple

The least common multiple of a set of monomials is the smallest multiple which is common among each of the numbers or monomials.

Example: Find the least common multiple of these monomials: 36d, 18de, 45d²e

Solution: Use a factor tree to find the prime factorization of each. Then find the largest amount of each different factor among all three. Finally, multiply these terms together for the least common multiple.

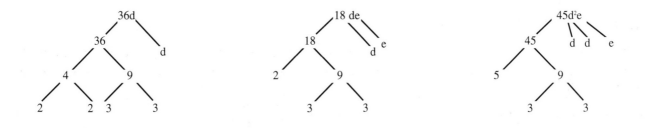

Answer: The least common multiple would be 2 x 2 x 3 x 3 x 5 x d x d x e = 180d²e.

❑ Equivalent Fractions

Equivalent fractions are fractions which are equal to one another.

Example: Are ¹/₂ and ⁵/₁₀ equivalent fractions?

Solution: ¹/₂ is in its simplest form, but ⁵/₁₀ can be reduced.

$$\frac{5 \div 5}{10 \div 10} = \frac{1}{2}$$

Answer: Since ¹/₂ = ¹/₂, the fractions are equivalent.

❏ Adding and Subtracting Mixed Numbers

The most important thing to remember when adding or subtracting fractions is that they must have common denominators.

Example: $36 \frac{1}{2}$ **=** $36 \frac{5}{10}$
$- 18 \frac{2}{5}$ $- 18 \frac{4}{10}$

                                       Answer: $18 \frac{1}{10}$

Need to borrow (regroup)

Example: $24 \frac{3}{8}$ **=** $24 \frac{6}{16}$ **=** $23 \frac{22}{16}$
$- 16 \frac{8}{16}$ $- 26 \frac{8}{16}$ $- 16 \frac{8}{16}$

                                           Answer: $7 \frac{14}{16}$
                                           Reduced: $7 \frac{7}{8}$

❏ Solving Equations Involving Rational Numbers

Equations were introduce on page 84. The addition and subtraction equations in this section, however, are somewhat more challenging because they contain decimals and fractions.

Example: *Addition Equation*   *Inverse Step—Subtraction*

             $m + 6.3 = 12.2$ Solution: $m + 6.3 = 12.2$
                                                    $- 6.3$ $- 6.3$

                                       Answer: $m = 5.9$

Example: *Subtraction Equation*   *Inverse Step—Addition*

             $m - 1 \frac{3}{4} = 5 \frac{3}{4}$ Solution: $m - 1 \frac{3}{4} = 5 \frac{3}{4}$
                                                   $+ 1 \frac{3}{4} + 1 \frac{3}{4}$

                          Answer: $m = 6 \frac{6}{4} = 7 \frac{2}{4}$
                          Reduced: $m = 7 \frac{2}{4} = 7 \frac{1}{2}$

❏ Sequences

Sequences are just lists of numbers, usually with some type of pattern driving the sequence. If you can learn the pattern for a sequence of numbers, then you can continue creating more numbers to build onto the list.

Example: Given this sequence of numbers: 3, 6, 9, 12, _____, _____, _____, name the missing numbers.

Answer: The pattern shows that three is added to the previous number to find the next term; therefore, the missing terms must be 15, 18, and 21.

❏ Multiplying Positive and Negative Decimals

When multiplying positive and negative decimals, first remember the rules for multiplying positive and negative integers. Although the rational number system is involved now, the integer rules still apply.

positive x positive = positive   *negative x positive = negative*
positive x negative = negative   *negative x negative = positive*

Also, do not forget that when multiplying decimals together, the number of digits to the right of the decimal in the numerals being multiplied indicates where the decimal should be placed in the final answer.

Examples:

-12.6	126	-.126	1.26
x 3.2	x 3.2	x -3.2	x -3.2
-40.32	403.2	.4032	-4.032

❏ Multiplying and Dividing Fractions

When multiplying or dividing fractions, it is not necessary to find common denominators.
To multiply fractions, multiply the numerators together and then multiply the denominators together.

Example: $\frac{2}{3} \times \frac{6}{7} = \frac{12}{21}$

Answer: $\frac{12}{21}$ reduces to $\frac{4}{7}$

To divide fractions, multiply the reciprocal (flip the fraction over) of the second fraction, and then follow the directions for multiplying.

Example: $\frac{2}{3} \div \frac{6}{7} = \frac{2}{3} \times \frac{7}{6}$

Answer: $\frac{14}{18}$ which reduces to $\frac{7}{9}$

❏ Using Scientific Notation

Scientific notation is often used when the numbers become too long and cumbersome. For example, the following number, 18,000,000,000,000,000,000,000,000, is very difficult to read. Scientific notation allows us to make it more manageable. Remember these two easy tricks about how to use scientific notation:

1. The decimal point is being moved to the left or right.
2. The decimal must be placed so that there is exactly one digit to the left of the decimal, and this number is multiplied by 10 to a certain power. (The power is determined by the number of places the decimal had to be moved.)

Example: Change 18,000,000,000,000,000,000,000,000 to scientific notation.

Answer: $18{,}000{,}000{,}000{,}000{,}000{,}000{,}000{,}000. = 1.8 \times 10^{25}$

Example: Change .0000000000123 to scientific notation.

Answer: $.0000000000123 = 1.23 \times 10^{-11}$

❏ Variables on Both Sides of an Equation

To solve an equation, simplify the sentence until an answer is derived that replaces the variable in the equation. If there are variables on both sides of the equal sign in an equation, the first step to solving must be to get all of the variables on one side of the equation and all of the numbers on the other side. After this is done, use the necessary inverse operation to find an answer for the variable.

Example: $2x + 3 = 5x - 18$

Solution:	$2x$	$+ 3$	$=$	$5x$	-18	
		$- 3$	$=$		$- 3$	Step #1
	$2x$		$=$	$5x$	$- 21$	
	$- 5x$			$- 5x$		Step #2
	$- 3x$		$=$		$- 21$	
	$\div$	-3		$\div$	-3	Step #3
Answer:	x		$=$		7	

❏ Solving Multi-Step Equations

The following equation is an example of a multi-step equation. As shown, one of the first things to do in a multi-step equation is to get all of the numbers together and all of the variables together. When more steps are involved in the equation, this task becomes slightly more difficult.

Example: $\dfrac{5x - 1}{3} = 33$

Solve for x: Step #1—Multiply both sides by three
to eliminate the fraction.

$$\frac{5x - 1}{3} \times 3 = 33 \times 3$$

	$5x - 1 =$	99	
	$+ 1$	$+ 1$	Step #2
	$5x$	$= 100$	
	$\div 5$	$\div 5$	Step #3
Answer:	$x =$	20	

❑ Graphing on a Number Line

After an equation or inequality is solved, another way to represent the answer to the problem is to mark its position on a number line. The following symbols are used for representation on a number line:

$x = a\ number$ (Mark a closed circle over that number on the number line.)

$x \leq a\ number$ (Mark a closed circle over that number, and draw a shaded arrow pointing to the left, representing all of the numbers less than that number.)

$x \geq a\ number$ (Mark a closed circle over that number, and draw a shaded arrow pointing to the right, representing all of the numbers greater than that number.)

$x < a\ number$ (Mark an open circle over the number, and draw a shaded arrow pointing to the left.)

$x > a\ number$ (Mark an open circle over the number, and draw a shaded arrow pointing to the right.)

Examples:

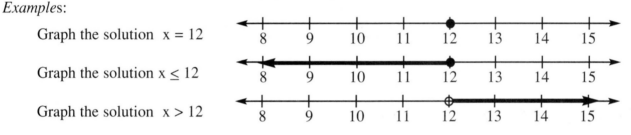

Graph the solution $x = 12$

Graph the solution $x \leq 12$

Graph the solution $x > 12$

❑ Graphing on the Cartesian Coordinate System

The Cartesian Coordinate System consists of two number lines, one running horizontally, called the *x-axis*, and one running vertically, called the *y-axis*. These two number lines intersect at a common point called the origin, which is located at (0, 0). To locate other points, ordered pairs are used, which are sets of two numbers, each containing the x value and the y value. Below, is an example of graphed numbers.

Hint: When graphing the numbers, remember that the first number is always the x value (so move horizontally first) and the second value is the y value (so move up or down for the second step).

A (3, 2)

B (-2, 3)

C (0, 0)

D (-1, -4)

E (3, -4)

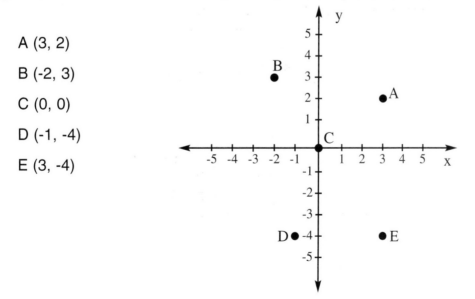

❏ Graphing Linear Equations

To graph a linear equation, calculate some ordered pairs, graph them, and then connect a line through the points. To find the ordered pairs, first create a linear equation. Then choose four values for x. Next, using the values for x, replace the x values in the equation, and solve for the y values. Finally, using the four ordered pairs, graph and connect the points.

Example: Graph the linear equation: $y = 2x + 1$

Solution: Make a table, choose four x values, solve for y, write the ordered pairs, and then graph.

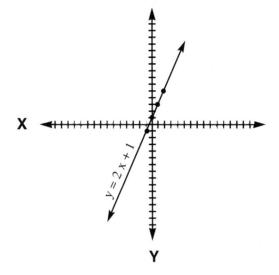

x	y = 2x + 1	y	(x, y)
-1	y = 2(-1) + 1	-1	(-1, -1)
0	y = 2(0) + 1	1	(0, 1)
1	y = 2(1) + 1	3	(1, 3)
2	y = 2(2) + 1	5	(2, 5)

❏ Solving Systems of Equations

A system of equations is used when there is more than one equation graphed on the same set of axes. The answer to a system is the point of intersection.

Example: Find the solution to the system:

$$y = 2x + 1$$
$$y = -x + 4$$

Solution:

Step #1—Make a table of values to find ordered pairs for each line.

y = 2x + 1	y = -x + 4
(-1, -1)	(-1, 5)
(0, 1)	(0, 4)
(1, 3)	(1, 3)
(2, 5)	(2, 2)

Step #2—Graph each of the lines on the same pair of axes.

Step #3—The point of intersection is the answer.

Answer: (1, 3)

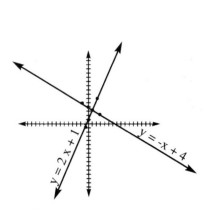

❑ Ratios as Fractions

A ratio is simply a comparison of one amount to another amount. Therefore, if you had a bag of 16 marbles (4 white, 7 blue, and 5 red) you could make a comparison with the marbles by using ratios. To turn a ratio into a fraction, use the first item being compared as the numerator and the second item as the denominator.

Example: Write the ratio of red marbles to blue marbles in fractional form.

Solution: 5 red : 7 blue = $^5/_7$

Example: Write the ratio of white marbles to total marbles in fractional form.

Solution: 4 white : 16 total = $^4/_{16}$ . . . reduced = $^1/_4$

❑ Solving Proportions

Proportions are two ratios set equal to each other. Therefore, they are equivalent fractions. To solve proportions, start with two ratios that are set equal to one another, with one of the ratios missing a numerator or denominator. Find a correct answer for that missing number which will make these ratios (fractions) equivalent. To find this number, cross multiply, and solve the resulting equation as seen below.

Example: $^x/_3 = ^4/_6$

Solution: Cross Multiply. $6x$ =   12

          Divide. $÷6$ $÷6$

Answer: x =   2   (therefore . . . $^2/_3 = ^4/_6$)

❑ Changing Decimals to Fractions to Percents

Whether a number is in the form of a decimal, fraction, or percent, it can always be converted into one or both of the other forms.

From decimal to fraction—Understanding place value after the decimal is the key to changing decimals to fractions.

1	.01	.001	.0001	.00001
10th	100th	1000th	10,000th	100,000th etc. . . .

Examples:

    $.9 = ^9/_{10}$ $.91 = ^{91}/_{100}$ $1.903 = 1 ^{903}/_{1000}$

From fraction to decimal—If your fraction is in the form of 10th, 100th, 1000th, etc., the change from fraction to decimal is just the opposite from the examples above. Otherwise, for any fraction, simply use division to determine what is the decimal equivalent.

Examples:

$$\frac{2}{5} = .4$$

$$\begin{array}{r} 0.4 \\ 5{\overline{)2.0}} \\ -2\,0 \\ \hline 0 \end{array}$$

$$\frac{3}{4} = .75$$

$$\begin{array}{r} 0.75 \\ 4{\overline{)3.00}} \\ -2\,8 \\ \hline 20 \\ 20 \\ \hline 0 \end{array}$$

From decimal to percent—A decimal is a percent when multiplied by 100. Therefore, by moving the decimal two places to the right (which is what happens when multiplying by 100), a decimal is made into a percent.

Examples: .63 = 63%   .6 = 60%   .06 = 6%

From percent to decimal—A percent is a decimal when divided by 100. Therefore, by moving the decimal two places to the left (which is what happens when dividing by 100), a percent is made into a decimal.

Examples: 72% = .72   12.6% = .126   2% = .02

❏ Solving Percent Problems

Percent problems usually need some simple mathematical transformations in order to solve them. These common key words associated with their mathematical symbols should help ease the look of some percent "story problems."

　　"of" *means* multiply
　　"What number" or "Some number" *means* use a variable
　　"%" *means* switch the number back to the useful decimal form
　　"is" *means* equals
Example: What number is 30% of 60?
　　n = .30 x 60
　　n = 18
Example: The number 20 is what percent of 60?

$$\frac{20}{60} = n\% \times \frac{60}{60}$$

$$\overline{.333} = n\%$$
$$33.\overline{3}\% = n$$

❏ Finding Percent Increase and Percent Decrease

Stores are always changing the prices of items: 25% markdown, 10% markup, an item decreased from $5.99 to $4.99, etc. Suppose two stores have the same item marked down.

　　Store #1: Pants—regularly $19.99. Take 25% off.

　　Store #2: Pants—regularly $20.99. Sale price $13.99.

Which store is giving the better percentage discount? Which store has the better price?
To find the percent decrease from Store #2, subtract the sale price from the original price: $20.99 – $13.99 = $7.00. Then divide the discount amount by the original price ($7.00 ÷ $20.99 = .333492139 or .3335, rounded out to four places). Finally, take this answer and multiply it by 100. The answer will be the percent decrease. The answer is 33.35%.

To find the percent increase of two amounts, begin by subtracting the original price from the new price. Then divide this answer (the amount of increase) by the original price. Finally, multiply this answer by 100, to represent the percent of markup.

❑ Frequency Tables, and Stem and Leaf Plots

Frequency tables, and stem and leaf plots are two methods for organizing data. Here is a list of data which, below, has been organized into each of the different forms.

Data: 10, 10, 12, 15, 16, 17, 17, 17, 19, 20, 25, 25, 25, 30, 31, 31, 31, 31

Frequency Table		
Number	Tally	Frequency
10	II	2
12	I	1
15	I	1
16	I	1
17	III	3
19	I	1
20	I	1
25	III	3
30	I	1
31	IIII	4

Stem and Leaf Plot	
1	0, 0, 2, 5, 6, 7, 7, 7, 9
2	0, 5, 5, 5
3	0, 1, 1, 1, 1

Other methods of organizing data include the scatter plot and box and whiskers diagram.

❑ Finding the Mean, Median, and Mode in a Set of Data

The mean in a set of data is an average. The median of a group of numbers is the exact middle number when the numbers are arranged from smallest to largest. The mode is the number which occurs most frequently. Below, the mean, median, and mode are shown for the data used above.

Mean: $\dfrac{10 + 10 + 12 + 15 + 16 + 17 + 17 + 17 + 19 + 20 + 25 + 25 + 25 + 30 + 31 + 31 + 31 + 31}{18}$

Mean = $382 \div 18 = 21.\overline{2}$

Median: In this case, there are two numbers in the middle. Therefore, we must take an average of these two numbers. 19 and 20 are in the middle, so, $\dfrac{19 + 20}{2} = 19.5$

Median = 19.5

Mode: There are four 31s. Therefore, 31 occurs the most often.

Mode = 31

❑ Factorials, Permutations, and Combinations

Factorials, permutations, and combinations are tools which help us find our sample space when dealing with probability.

Factorials—A factorial is a number followed by an exclamation point. It tells a person to start at the number shown and multiply down to one. The product is the answer. (Note: 0! is equal to 1.)

$$n! = n \times (n - 1) \times (n - 2) \times \ldots \times 1$$

Example: $5! = 5 \times 4 \times 3 \times 2 \times 1 = 120$

Permutations—A permutation is like a partial factorial. Begin at the number n and only multiply down as many numbers as r says.

$$P(n, r)$$

Examples: $P(7, 3) = 7 \times 6 \times 5 = 210$

$P(5, 5) = 5 \times 4 \times 3 \times 2 \times 1 = 120$

Combinations—A combination is a permutation divided by r!.

$$C(n, r) = \frac{P(n, r)}{r!}$$

Example: $C(7, 3) = \frac{P(7, 3)}{3!} = \frac{7 \times 6 \times 5}{3 \times 2 \times 1} = \frac{210}{6} = 35$

❑ Basic Probability

Probability is the chance that something will happen. In mathematics, the probability of an event occurring is found by dividing the number of favorable outcomes by the total number of possible outcomes.

$$\text{Probability} = \frac{\text{Number of favorable outcomes}}{\text{Total number of outcomes}}$$

Example: In a drawer, there are four red socks, three blue socks, and ten white socks.

Without looking, what is the probability that you will choose a red sock?

P(red) = 4/17

What is the probability of choosing a red or blue sock?

P(red or blue) = 7/17

What is the probability of choosing a green sock?

P(green) = 0/17 = 0

❑ Vertical, Complementary, and Supplementary Angles

Vertical angles are formed when two lines intersect. The angles opposite each other are called vertical angles, and they are congruent.

    Example:

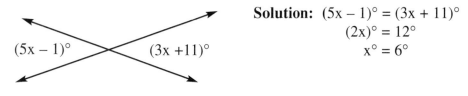

Solution: $(5x - 1)° = (3x + 11)°$
$$(2x)° = 12°$$
$$x° = 6°$$

The first angle is $5(6) - 1 = 29°$.   The second angle is $3(6) + 11 = 29°$.

Complementary angles are two angles whose sum is 90°.

    Example:

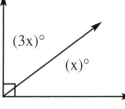

Solution: $(3x + x)° = 90°$
$$(4x)° = 90°$$
$$x° = 22.5°$$

The larger angle is $3x = 3(22.5) = 67.5°$.
The smaller angle is $x = 22.5°$.

Supplementary angles are two angles whose sum is 180°.

    Example:

Solution: $(2x - 5)° + (3x + 30)° = 180°$
$$(5x + 25)° = 180°$$
$$(5x)° = 155°$$
$$x° = 31°$$

The larger angle is $(3x + 30)° = 3(31) + 30 = 123°$.
The smaller angle is $(2x - 5)° = 2(31) - 5 = 57°$.

❑ Angles Formed by a Transversal and Parallel Lines

When dealing with angles formed by a transversal and parallel lines, note the following rules:

- Alternate interior angles are congruent. ($\angle 3 \cong \angle 5$, $\angle 4 \cong \angle 6$)
- Alternate exterior angles are congruent. ($\angle 1 \cong \angle 7$, $\angle 2 \cong \angle 8$)
- Vertical angles are congruent. ($\angle 1 \cong \angle 3$, $\angle 2 \cong \angle 4$, $\angle 5 \cong \angle 7$, $\angle 6 \cong \angle 8$)
- Interior angles on the same side are supplementary. ($\angle 4 + \angle 5 = 180°$, $\angle 6 + \angle 3 = 180°$)
- Exterior angles on the same side are supplementary. ($\angle 1 + \angle 8 = 180°$, $\angle 2 + \angle 7 = 180°$)

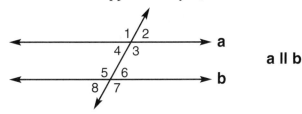

a ‖ b

❑ Missing Angles in Triangles

The three angles of a triangle add up to 180 degrees. Therefore, if two of the interior angles are known, the third angle can be found by adding the two angle degrees and subtracting the sum from 180°. This difference represents the missing angle measure. In order to solve some problems, an algebraic equation is required.

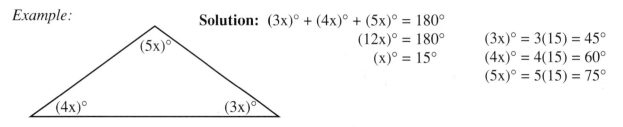

Example:

Solution: $(3x)° + (4x)° + (5x)° = 180°$
$(12x)° = 180°$ $(3x)° = 3(15) = 45°$
$(x)° = 15°$ $(4x)° = 4(15) = 60°$
$(5x)° = 5(15) = 75°$

❑ Corresponding Parts of Congruent Triangles Are Congruent

If two triangles are congruent (same shape, same size), then the parts which match up from one triangle to the other (corresponding parts) will be congruent (the same measure).

Example: If $\triangle$ XYZ is congruent to $\triangle$ MNL, then

Congruent segments are:

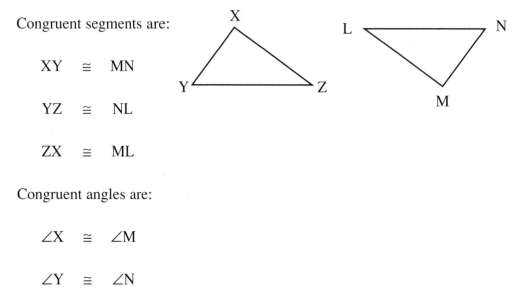

XY $\cong$ MN

YZ $\cong$ NL

ZX $\cong$ ML

Congruent angles are:

$\angle$X $\cong$ $\angle$M

$\angle$Y $\cong$ $\angle$N

$\angle$Z $\cong$ $\angle$L

❑ Writing Conditional Statements

Conditional statements are sentences which contain an **if** and a **then**.

Example: **If** you add two plus two, **then** you will get a sum of four.
(This is a true conditional statement.)

Example: **If** you see clouds, **then** it must rain.
(This conditional statement is not true, because it does not have to rain whenever there are clouds in the sky.)

❏ Common Formulas

The *area* of a figure is the amount of square units inside of the figure itself. The perimeter of a figure is the sum of all of the surrounding sides.

- Area of a Rectangle = base x height

2

4

4 x 2 = 8 square units

- Perimeter of a Rectangle = 2(length) + 2(width)

3

5

2(5) + 2(3) = 16 units

- Area of a Square = side x side

4

4

4 x 4 = 16 square units

- Area of a Triangle = ¹/₂ base x height

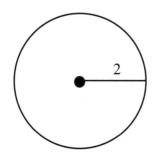

7

4

¹/₂ (4) x 7 = 14 square units

- Area of a Parallelogram = base x height

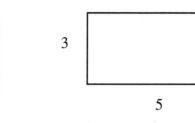

4

6

6 x 4 = 24 square units

- Area of a Trapezoid = ¹/₂ x height x (top base + bottom base)

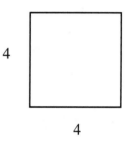

6

4

8

¹/₂ (4) x (6 + 8) = 28 square units

- Area of a Circle = π x radius² or π r²

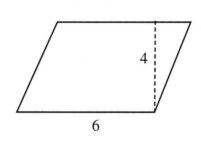

2

3.14 x 2² = 12.56

- Circumference of a Circle = π x diameter or π d

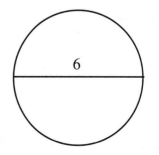

6

3.14 x 6 = 18.84

#2039 Pre-Algebra Brain Teasers

Amazing Face (I)—*page 4*

8	4	7	24	8	4	15	3	5	9	18	2	8	15	31	7	11	12	3
6	2	7	6	18	3	33				1	9	7	10	26	6	5	4	9
2	7	9	27	0	6			8		9	7	26	31	5	15	8	5
8	6	4	2			12	3			6	8	10	12	4	16	18	2
0	8	7	6			10	4	3	4	8	10	9	7	8	9	10	7	8
5	5	3	26	1	2		8	2	4	7	15	2	11	19	3	21	22	3
14	8	5	6	7	8	9		10	6	7	15	6	31	2	0	10	13	4
11	2	7	12	18	6	9	16		15	5	25	4	2	0	3	11	17	8
27	1	6	8	5	0	5	18		14	23	4	5	31	27	2	16	21	2
0	26	7	9	28	6	5	5	13		29	9	6	4	26	5	13	15	4
3	27	8	19	2	3	8	13	8		32	8	2	11	12	6	19	28	1
9	6	5	7	22	0	7	15	4		4	7	7	41	52	5	27	29	0

Amazing Face (II)—*page 5*

0	-3	7	-52	1	-3	-3	15	-48	43	7			-8	21	-5	1	-1	9	-6	-4	-16
-27	-5	4	-6	11	28	11	2	1	24	-19		-15		-3	3	-13	52	-10	2	17	-5
14	-3	0	9	-41	36	9	-2	2	-17	18		15	-14		0	20	-1	4	22	-4	8
-5	10	9	28	17	8	1	1	54	13		8	-14	17		11	-10	3	-8			8
-4	20	8	2	3	32	-1	13	-9			-3	14	-14		-4	4	-15		12	-13	
-3	-19	7	-2	30	33	52	1	5	-5	-2	9	-14	11	-10				-9	9	11	
-2	-18	6	9	2	8	-4	11	51	-4	3	20	33	-9	-7	-2	-35	8	59	-43	0	
-1	-17	5	1	29	-46	0	-3	-53	10	-10	-4	-34	-3	0	21	19	1	43	57	-8	14
0	16	4	13	1	9	-2	1	-52	-1	1	-5	22	17	8	-35	0	6	-5	-2	7	-12

Name That Term—*page 6*

1. associative
2. identity
3. commutative
4. brackets
5. parentheses
6. variable
7. equation
8. open sentence
9. expression
10. order of operations
11. properties
12. distributive
13. simplify
14. inverse
15. inequality

"Express" Yourself—*page 7*

Lipstick Lady—*page 8*
She was trying to make up her mind.
Writer's Dilemma—*page 9*
Sometimes they have to eat their words.

A Really "Pig" Show—*page 10*
Ham it up!

A Sensible Solution—*page 11*
Ribbit

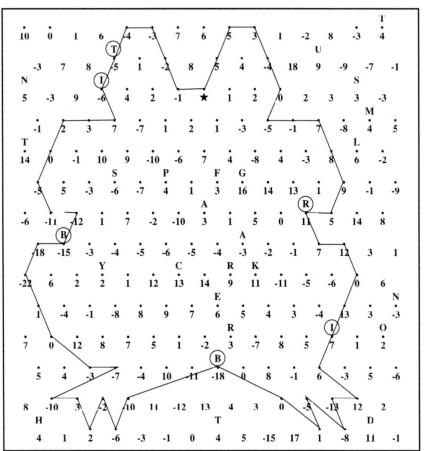

"Spl-Integers"—*pages 12 and 13*

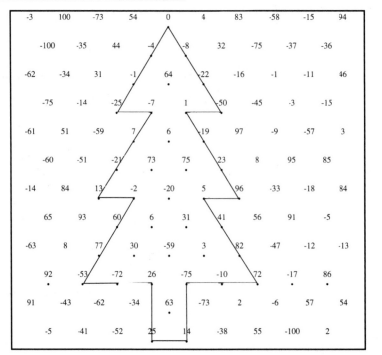

A Military Matter—*page 14*
He thought he would be a good drill sergeant.

Puzzling Problem—*page 15*

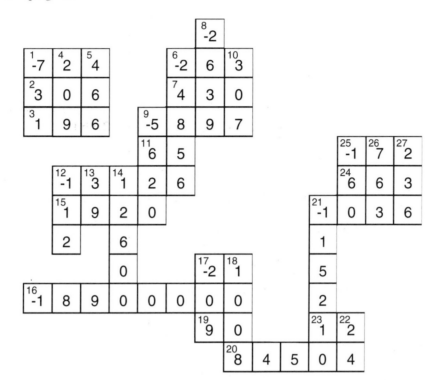

Too Fast!—*page 16*
It must have been the hurri-cane.
Lovesick—*page 17*
She takes the stares.
A Croaking Crook—*page 18*

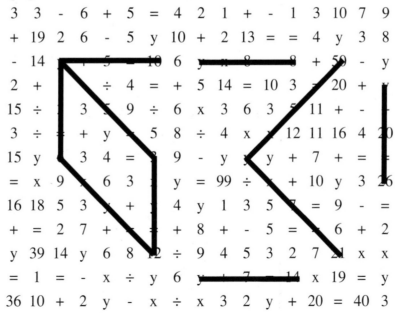

It kermitted a crime!

The Wacky Werewolf—*page 19*

```
y  +  >  20  <  y  -  21  >  48  36  <  -  16  17  x
x  26  y  ÷  y  +  18  <  34  +  4  >  5  49  ÷  x
<  <  x  1  -  8  ÷  27  >  x  <  y  ÷  2  >  3
y  13  8  <  6  >  20  3  19  ÷  y  +  x  7  ÷  63
-  ÷  <  -  <  40  x  <  >  9  x  7  6  7  ÷  y
0  y  6  +  5  y  y  +  5  <  6  <  15  19  <  +
>  y  ÷  <  ÷  2  >  x  8  18  <  12  24  51  3  30
4  25  x  3  12  18  40  ÷  6  7  67  -  <  +  27  <
>  >  <  >  y  -  3  +  8  <  >  y  +  6  >  37
16  12  12  x  ÷  <  31  >  x  -  18  ÷  -  9  14  <
+  +  11  +  3  16  +  x  y  +  +  13  x  +  y  21
y  <  >  ÷  >  x  18  ÷  <  23  3  y  +  16  >  26
<  >  y  x  4  >  32  10  49  +  y  x  22  <  2  >
```

Wrong Howliday

Follow the Divisibility Road—*page 20*

1. 4
2. 26
3. 46
4. 10
5. 15
6. 36
7. 17
8. 35
9. 22
10. 102
11. 49
12. 39
13. 45
14. 15
15. 27
16. 19
17. 105
18. -1
19. 208
20. 5

Start
↓

$6 + c$	$3c + d$	$e + d$	$14a + e$
↓			
$23 + a + b$ → $-(bcd - 14)$	$2d + a$	$be - d$
	↓		
$e - c$ ← $d - c$	$a + b + c + d + e$ → $100 - ac$
↓		↑	↓
$4d + 2b$ → $e + 2b$ → $37 + c$	$(d - a)^2$
			↓
$3e$	$b + c + 73$	$23 - c$	$2e + d + 5$
			↓
$12 + b - a$	$c - 49$	$b + 11 - c$ ← $5(e - 2b)$
		↓	
$c - b$	$a + b + 19$	$3(a + d)$	$3b$
		↓	
$17 + c$	$e - a$	$d + e + c$	$e + d - 3$
		↓	
$a + 4$	$c - a + 2$ ← $a + 104$	$a + b + c$
	↓		
$e - d$ ← $d \times e \times b$	$-6c$	$2b + 2c$

Finish

Time for a Treat—*pages 21 and 22*
When left in your pocket, it becomes hot chocolate!

A Penny for Your Thoughts—*page 23*
. . . is a man who makes no cents.

Surprise Dish—*page 24*
Surprise! It's tuna casserole.

From a Lawyer's Lips—*page 25*
Oh, it's just another brief case.

The Bacon Company—*page 26*
Because his name was Chris B. Meat.

Term Search—*page 27*

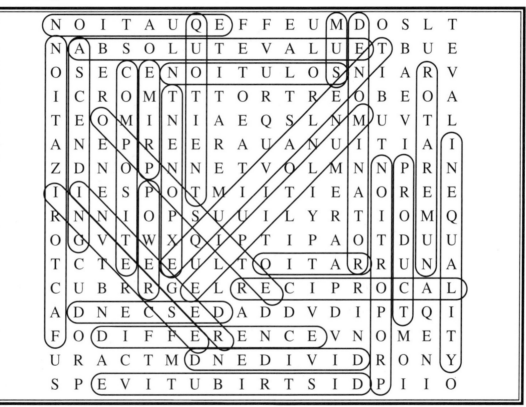

A "Sharking" Discovery—*page 28*
It was a man eating shark.

The Problem with Pachyderms—*page 29*
Offer him your pillow.

"Stair" Crazy—*page 30*
He thought that she had fallen for him.

Rabbit Riddle—*page 31*
My, this is definitely a hare-raising experience!

Pilot Puzzle—*page 32*
A dirty double-crosser!

Duck Cookies—*page 33*
A box of quackers

A Dating Disaster—*page 34*
Rick A. Mortis

Reggae Frog—*page 35*
Don't worry, be hoppy!

Words of Wisdom—*page 36*
Don't get hooked!

Go, Team, Go!—*page 37*
Buck-an-ears

Baby Genius—*page 38*
Because the baby said, "Polygon!"

You Are What You Drink—*page 39*
Sonny D. Light

Write Your Own Riddle—*page 40*
Question: Why did the surfer dude cross the ocean?

Answer: To get to the other tide

Smile!—*pages 41 and 42*

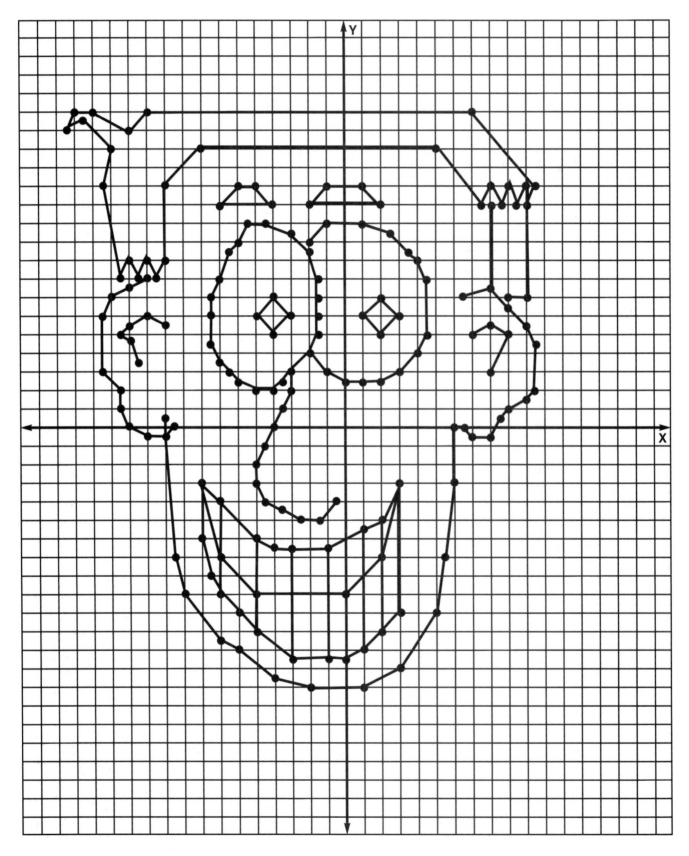

You Can Lead Them to Water . . .—*page 43*

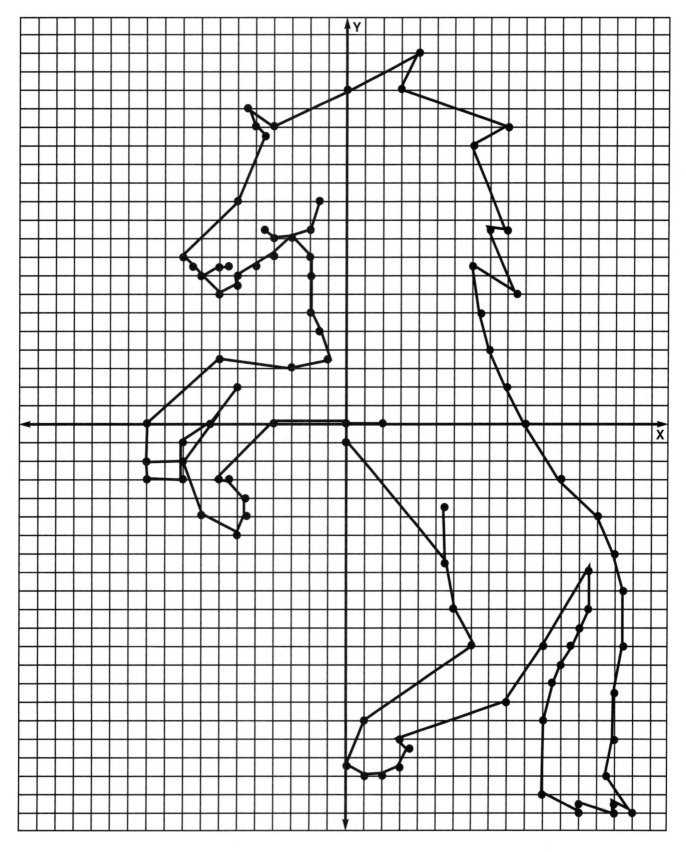

Largest Migrating Mammal—*page 45*

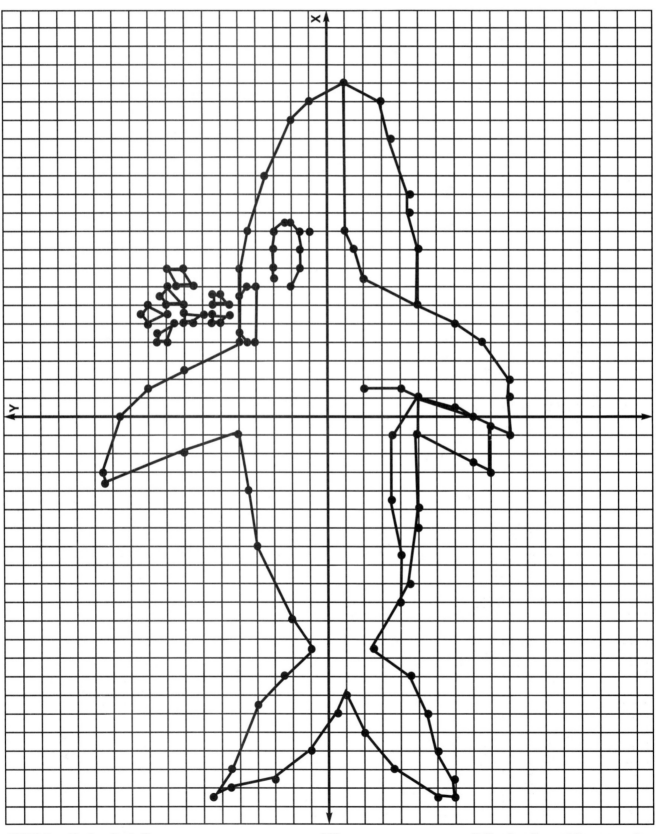

Crisscross—*page 47*
Orange you ready?

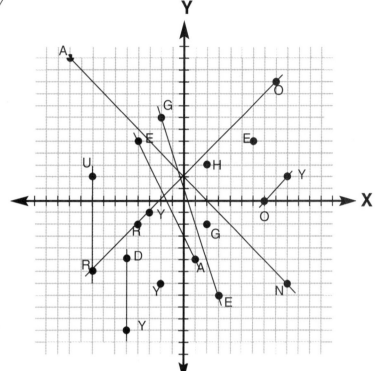

A Canine Question—*pages 48 and 49*
Scuby Diving

A Crossword Puzzle of Graphing Terms—*pages 50 and 51*

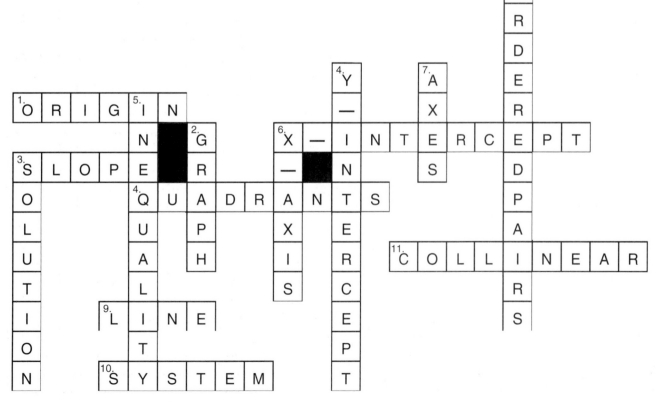

A Funny Feline—*page 52*

An Octo-Puss

The Very Best—*page 53*

Will E. Evermiss

Fractions, Decimals and Percents—*page 54*

They both love to (w)rap!

Don't Ruffle the Bird's Feathers—*page 55*

A lot of hoop-la and fan-fare!

Chow Time—*page 56*

Cream of Tweet

Pet-Pal Parlor—*pages 57 and 58*

I don't know—it's history anyway!

The Young Vampire—*page 59*

The girls necks-door.

No Rest for the Weary—*page 60*

Mt. Neverest

Doggy Diagnosis—*page 61*

I don't think it will develop into anything serious.

The Land Down Under—*page 62*

Outback

Stems	Leaves
4	7,
5	7, 8
6	2, 3, 3, 7
7	0, 4, 5, 9, 9,
8	0, 1, 3, 7, 8, 8
9	1, 1, 3, 3, 6, 6, 8
10	0, 0, 0

Number of leaves	Letter
1	O
2	U
4	T
5	B
6	A
7	C
3	K

Disguising Data Definitions—*pages 63 and 64*

1. range
2. median
3. mean
4. mode
5. stem and leaf plot
6. frequency table
7. tally
8. box and whiskers
9. outlier
10. data
11. upper quartile
12. survey
13. sample
14. scatter plot

```
M T R P E R Q U A R T I L F S U
T O Y E G N A R E U V U E R T P
E L C T R A A M G S E Q U E L P
T P N I A I O I N R Y R U Q M E
S F E L E D N D A R Q Y P U A R
U E U E E E O E M F E P N E Z Q
R L O Q D M E A N V E E D N F U
V S U A T O L P R E T T A C S A
Y T T E A M P U S P A C T Y A R
D M L R T A S L E Y L L A T M T
N A I F A S B L E T O E L A P I
S R E K S I H W D N A X O B L L
L A R T T C S S C A T R P L E E
F T O L P F A E L D N A M E T S
```

Heard It Through the Grapevine—*page 65*

We are raisin a bunch of grape kids!

Probably Probability—*page 66*

1. P (9) = 1/12 = .08
2. P (multiple of 2) = 6/12 = 1/2 = .50
3. P (even number) = 6/12 = 1/2 = .50
4. P (prime number) = 5/12 = .47
5. P (number < 8) = 7/12 = .58
6. P (factor of 8) = 4/12 = 1/3 = .33
7. P (orange) = 5/20 = 1/4 = .25
8. P (blue) = 4/20 = 1/5 = .20
9. P (not blue) = 16/20 = 4/5 = .80
10. P (white) = 0/20 = 0 = 0
11. P (1, heads) = 1/12 = .08
12. P (2, tails) = 1/12 = .08
13. P (6, heads or tails) = 1/6 = .17
14. P (even, tails) = 3/12 = 1/4 = .25
15. P (odd, heads or tails) = 1/2 = .50

Total: 4.79

Know the Terms—*page 67*

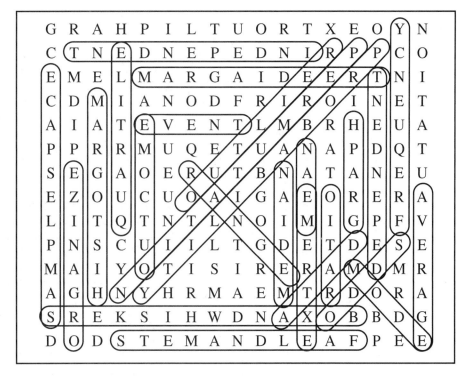

What's Left?—*page 68*

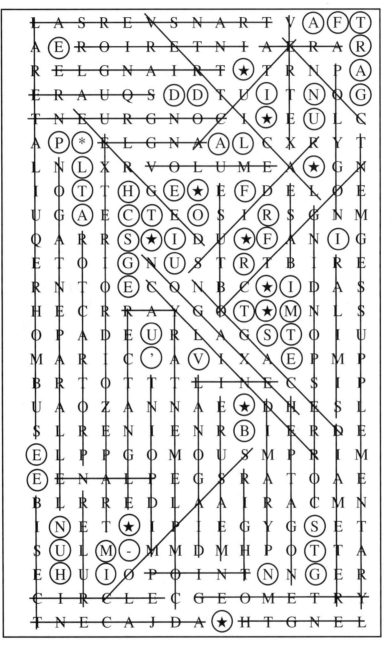

After adding up all the factors, I figure it must've been sum-thing.

Food for Thought—*page 69*
Fillet of Sole

The Square Team—*page 70*
Forty-Niners

Mystery Name—*page 71*
John John Son

Vacation Destination—*page 72*
The Rockies

All Aboard!—*page 73*
Train Your Brain

Shop 'Til You Drop—*page 74*
She kept charging up the credit card.

Speedy the Squirrel—*page 75*
It must've been nuts!

Check, please!—*page 76*
This is "egg"cellent!

A Painful Problem—*page 77*
M&M—eow!

Corny Acorns—*page 78*
Geometry (pronounced: "Gee I'm a tree!")